D0597149

Game of My Life

PHILADELPHIA EAGLES

MEMORABLE STORIES OF EAGLES FOOTBALL

ROBERT GORDON

SP
SPORTS
PUBLISHING
L.L.C.

SportsPublishingLLC.com

ISBN 13: 978-1-59670-229-5

Publishers: Peter L. Bannon and Joseph J. Bannon Sr.
Senior managing editor: Susan M. Moyer
Acquisitions editor: John Humenik
Developmental editor: Laura Podeschi
Art director: Dustin J. Hubbart
Interior design: Kathryn R. Holleman
Photo editor: Erin Linden-Levy

Sports Publishing L.L.C.
804 North Neil Street
Champaign, IL 61820
Phone: 1-877-424-2665
Fax: 217-363-2073
SportsPublishingLLC.com

Printed in the United States of America

Library of Congress Cataloging-in-Publication Data

Gordon, Bob (Robert)
  Game of my life. Philadelphia Eagles : memorable stories of Eagles football / Robert Gordon.
     p. cm.
  Includes bibliographical references and index.
  ISBN 978-1-59670-229-5 (hard cover : alk. paper)
  1. Philadelphia Eagles (Football team) 2. Football players--United States--Anecdotes. I. Title. II. Title: Philadelphia Eagles. III. Title: Memorable stories of Eagles football.

GV956.P44G67 2007
796.332'640974811--dc22
                              2007031755

CONTENTS

PREFACE

The true "Eagles Tradition" didn't start way back in 1933. Yes, the Philadelphia Eagles came into existence that year. But the Eagles Tradition ... well, that lagged a bit, at least the Eagles Tradition as we know it today. That tradition soars on the wings of Steve Van Buren, Chuck Bednarik, Pete Pihos, Tommy McDonald, Wilbert Montgomery, Reggie White, Donovan McNabb, Brian Dawkins, and similar stars. Unfortunately, players of that caliber didn't begin to pop up with any regularity in the City of Brotherly Love till the dawn of the '40s. We can roughly set the inception of the Eagles Tradition sometime around the time Earl "Greasy" Neale arrived to assume the role of head coach.

Frankly, in their first decade, the Eagles were a sorry squad. Their abysmal performances during the Depression years were doubly tough to swallow for Philadelphia sport fans, who were accustomed to the high bar set by the Philadelphia Athletics and the Frankford Yellow Jackets. Connie Mack's Philadelphia A's were the uncontested darlings of the Quaker City in that era. The A's established one of baseball's all-time dynasties during the Murderer's Row heyday. Every baseball fan knows of the legendary Yankees Murderers Row team. However, in 1929, '30, and '31, the Philadelphia A's, not NY's Murderer's Row, won the American League pennant. Led by future Hall of Famers Mickey Cochrane, Lefty Grove, Jimmy Foxx, and Al Simmons, the A's destroyed all comers, winning two of three World Series during that stretch.

The new-kid-on-the-block '33 Eagles also had to compete with the specter of the Frankford Yellow Jackets for the city's love and attention. The fledgling Birds had a tough gridiron act to follow because the Philadelphia Eagles were actually the second football franchise from Philadelphia. They were the first to represent Philadelphia, but they weren't the city's first NFL team. The Frankford Yellow Jackets hold that distinction. From its entrance into the NFL in 1924 till its 1931 NFL curtain call, the Frankford Yellow Jacket franchise insisted it was neither of nor for Philadelphia. The Yellow Jackets and their rooters were fiercely proud to represent only the Frankford section of Philadelphia. They were not the Philadelphia Yellow Jackets. The Yellow Jackets' business office, practice facility, and stadium (which the franchise built and funded itself—what a concept) were all located in their home 'hood of Frankford. Everything was funded by internal football operations. The Frankford franchise's identity and business affairs were entirely divorced from the city proper.

Despite their insularity, the Yellow Jackets' teams were shockingly successful. The Yellow Jackets' 69-45 won-lost record remains one of the NFL's loftier all-time marks for any franchise. In fact, back in 1926, the Yellow Jackets won the NFL championship—a feat the Philadelphia Eagles could not match till 1960. To this day, Frankford remains the only neighborhood team ever to win an NFL championship. Presumably they'll carry that distinction till football players are characters in books written by rabbits or, more likely, until pro football is replaced by Mad Max-like warriors battling over gasoline for their hometown fans.

But let's get back to the Philadelphia Eagles of 1933, the year of their NFL debut. When financial woes finally did the Yellow Jackets in, Philadelphia had an opening for a new football franchise. The City of Brotherly Love, the nation's third largest city at the time, represented an excellent potential market. The only problem with Philly was its Blue Laws. Up until 1933, it was against the law to play football on Sunday. That situation changed in 1933. How, you might ask, did the Frankford Yellow Jackets cope with the Blue Laws? They simply drew up a killer schedule. The Frankford boys spent each fall weekend playing a Saturday game in Philly, followed by an overnight train trip to destinations like Canton, where they squared off the following day, Sunday, against the same opponent.

In 1933, Pennsylvania found itself $30 million in debt. One city official estimated that allowing Sunday sports would add one and a quarter million bucks to the state coffers. Capitalism suddenly played rock to the scissors of religion, causing individuals to rethink and repeal the Blue Laws. Well, not *all* Sunday Blue Laws were scrapped, but the ones that prohibited Sunday football and its associated revenue were. Playing pro football on Sunday was no longer considered an affront to the Creator, whereas selling cars, for example, was—and is. Since Blue Laws continue to prohibit Sunday car sales, that activity presumably still bollixes the Divine Plan. In any event, in April 1933, playing football professionally on Sunday shed its mantle of immorality as swiftly, inscrutably, and unapologetically as eating fish on Friday when I was younger and Catholic.

Bye-bye Blue Laws, hello Eagles. All was not rosy, however. Playing home football games on Sunday unfortunately lent little succor to the Eagles' early success. The baby Birds lost their first regular-season NFL tilt against the established New York Giants 56-0. After that inauspicious start, the Eagles kept right on losing all the way till 1943. That's the year they finally posted a winning season. Philadelphia's log for its first decade of NFL play (from 1933 to 1942) was 23-82-4. The Eagles Tradition was not yet born, but it was gestating.

Even the team's first winning season record is tainted. In 1943, at the height of the Second World War, the Eagles combined forces with the Pittsburgh Steelers to fashion a 5-4-1 record. The following year, however, the Philly-Pittsburgh union was dismantled, and the Philadelphia Eagles came on like wildfire. That year, Steve Van Buren, one of the game's first superstars, arrived in Philadelphia via Louisiana State University, where he had been the blocking back for baseball star Alvin Dark. Van Buren broke virtually every NFL rushing record over his storied career. His arrival initiated a skein of six straight winning Eagles seasons. A host of legitimate stars like Ernie Steele, Bucko Kilroy, Vic Sears, Bosh Pritchard, Tommy Thompson, Pete Pihos, and others started a run of Eagles football greats that kicked off the Eagles Tradition.

When the '40s ended, the world had witnessed the dismantling of the Third Reich, a world war that caused the senseless death of 50 million human beings (25 million from the Soviet Union alone, along with 300,000 Americans), the invention and unleashing of the atomic bomb, the Berlin Airlift, the establishment of the state of Israel, and the start of the Cold War. Though no less a humanist than General George S. Patton once proclaimed, "Compared to war, all other forms of human endeavor shrink to insignificance," the Eagles overachieved during that war-ravaged decade. They rolled to a 70-39-4 log in the '40s. At the close of that crucial decade, the Eagles won two consecutive NFL championships. In doing so, they were the first and only team to shut out two opponents consecutively in NFL championship game competition. How's that for Eagles Tradition?

The Eagles have ignited Philly's fall weekends 1,046 times since their inception in 1933. Every one of those games has lit up somebody's life or kindled some treasured memory. I know the game I'll always remember. It was a "meaningless" season finale in 1971—meaningless in terms of history and meaningless in terms of the postseason chase, but very meaningful to me personally. The Eagles beat the Giants 41-28 that day in a game that the world and history would little note nor long remember. But I'll never forget that day.

You see, when I was a kid, my dad and I watched every Eagles game together—father and son bonding in the Eagles Tradition. We were at Franklin Field together on December 26, 1960, when the Eagles shocked the world and won their last NFL championship. We had season tickets the following year, too. Then I went off to high school. My school played its football games on Sunday. That's when my father lost his Eagles-game partner. I was crossing that threshold—the one kids cross when they start spending time with friends and shutting their dads out. From a dad's perspective, that prospect is like losing a right arm. From a kid's perspective, it's like—well, it's like nothing, no big deal. The thought never struck me at the time. It didn't strike me till years later, when my son stole my act.

I had graduated from college in 1970. My father and I had begun watching the Eagles together again, setting Sundays aside for some father-son quality time. But I was engaged. The next year, I would be moving away from my parents' neighborhood. I'd have a different life with new responsibilities and new demands. I contemplated all that data as I watched the game with my dad that day, sitting in that old house where I had grown up safe and secure. What was a meaningless gridiron contest to most of the world transformed over the years into a precious memory. That was the last time my father and I would be able to watch the Eagles together on a regular basis—the last time just the two of us would shut out the world and its woes for awhile just to enjoy each other's company. Yep, I remember that silly game: Eagles 41, Giants 28—Harold Jackson catching a long TD pass and the living room resonating with our shouts.

What memories do these Sunday contests hold for the warriors out there on the turf? What makes a particular Sunday stick out? What makes an Eagle or ex-Eagle look back on a particular game years later and call it the game of his life? Maybe it's the game where the camera catches a gesture. And maybe that gesture beams a wink and a nod across the airwaves to that player's father, watching the game half a continent away. That's why Vai Sikahema remembers one contest against the Giants so well. Maybe it's an insignificant game in which neither team has anything to gain, but a young offensive lineman goes head to head against the era's best defensive tackle and, when the gun ends the contest, the youngster has gained the star's respect and praise. That's why Jim Skaggs remembers an otherwise meaningless game against the Lions. Maybe it's the first game a native Texan defensive back enters the fray as part of the defensive unit. Dallas is slaughtering the Eagles at the time, but the rookie intercepts his first NFL pass and returns it for a Philly TD. That's the game Bill Bradley picks as the game of his life. Maybe it's the game in which an Eagles great plays with a broken jaw that's wired shut. He plays because the owner told him he must and he responds by scoring four TDs. Afterwards, the owner congratulates him and tells him they're going to break his jaw more often. That's the game Tommy McDonald picks as the game of his life. Maybe it's the game before which a real-deal Philadelphia Rocky talks with a kid in the park across from the Vet. The kid is wearing an Eagles jersey with this guy's number on it. The Eagle promises the kid that he's going to make a special play just for that kid and backs it up by causing a big fumble to ice the game. That's the contest Vince Papale chooses as his most memorable.

You'll find out what games Eagles stars old and new remember as the games of their lives. Players featured in the book span every era of the Eagles Tradition from the '40s to the present. Sadly, three of the guys I interviewed for this book, Ernie Steele, Vic Sears, and Andre Waters, passed away over the course of the project. Ernie Steele, a star of the '40s, made one of the biggest plays in Eagles history. Ernie intercepted a ball late in a game played in a driving blizzard. That game was the 1948 NFL Championship, and Ernie's heroics iced the Philadelphia win. Lineman Vic Sears was one of the offensive-line rocks on both the 1948 and 1949 championship teams. Andre Waters' death shocked the entire sport world. About two weeks after Andre and I spoke, he tragically and inexplicably took his own life. As of this writing, concussions Andre suffered in NFL competition are suspected as contributory. Meanwhile, Ted Johnson, a longtime Patriots star, is fingering football concussions as the culprit for a host of neurological problems—everything from premature Alzheimer's disease to depression.

Current stars Brian Dawkins and defensive backfield mate Lito Sheppard weigh in with their most memorable games. All-time greats like Chuck Bednarik, Tommy McDonald, Bill Bergey, Dick Vermeil, Seth

Joyner, Bill Bradley, Tim Brown, and Claude Humphrey chime in as well. Media mavens Merrill Reese, Bill Campbell, and Dave Spadaro carve out their favorite memories as well as a contingent of ex-Eagles players who morphed into media types, like Vai Sikahema, Mike Quick, Garry Cobb, and Brian Baldinger. A cache of talented but less flashy performers like Wade Key, Chuck Weber, John Outlaw, Greg Brown, and David Alexander hold their particular prisms to the past as well as local legends such as William Thomas, Frank LeMaster, Ben Hawkins, and Keith Jackson.

All in all, 31 Eagles personalities—players, coaches, and announcers —share the ins and outs of the games of their lives. Their stories pay homage to the Eagles Tradition—a tradition every Eagles fan has helped thrive.

"OK, FANS, WHY SHOULD PLAYERS HAVE ALL THE FUN?"

In closing, if you have memories to share about an Eagles game, an Eagles event, or an Eagles encounter that holds special meaning, e-mail your story in 400 words or less to the book's author, Robert Gordon, who handles the "Ever-Green" column on the Eagles' website, at Eagles-evergreen@hotmail.com. The best entries, along with a profile and photo of the fan submitting the story, are published on the "Ever-Green" page of the Eagles' website.

Chapter 1

ERNIE STEELE

"SO, WHAT WAS THE GAME OF YOUR LIFE?"

Ernie Steele: "I had many a fond memory in those years of playing football. Having the opportunity to play professional football back east like I did in a place like Philadelphia was something I never expected as a youngster. I was fortunate for having that opportunity, and I'm grateful and happy for it. I came to Philadelphia at a trying time, what with the big war going on and the Eagles not exactly being a very fine team. Things started to turn around for the Eagles, though, when Steve Van Buren showed up. That fellow could run with the best of them—toughest man to tackle I've ever seen. We had some big games in that march from being a bad team to being champs. I remember a game I played as a Steagle against the Giants when we were down 14-0 and came back to win. [The game he's referring to was October 9, 1942, at Shibe Park, Philadelphia, when the Steagles beat the Giants 28-14.] There were 10 fumbles or so in that game. I remember Jack Hinkle intercepting a pass and running it all the way back up the field. [Hinkle's interception was a 90-yarder.]

"Then we gave the Giants and Redskins a real thumping near the start of the 1948 season. I'll bet Philly fans nowadays don't remember anything about these games. We beat the Giants and Redskins back to back 45-0. How about them apples? They were sure enough thrilling, both of those games. And, personally speaking, I could never forget my

1

very first pro game as an Eagle. I ran a punt back for a touchdown. It was an 89-yarder and quite a thrill for a young fellow new to the league. But if you're asking me about the game of my life, how could I pick any other game than that 1948 championship game? First of all, that was my final football game ever. And second, well, I was a team player, and I'd have been happy if we had won without me doing anything special, but as it turns out, I did do something pretty special in that game. I made, I guess, the biggest play of my life. So, that's my pick for the game of my life, as you call it. And that game would be the one we played in Shibe Park in Philadelphia against the Chicago Cardinals for the NFL championship."

Ernie Steele is not a household name in Philadelphia. That's a travesty because Ernie was instrumental in Philly's climb from the NFL basement to the NFL's first postwar dynasty. Ernie Steele starred for the Washington University Huskies in college. As Ernie tells it, he wasn't playing pro ball when the Philadelphia Eagles picked him up off the docks in 1942 and signed him to a humble NFL contract. He arrived in Philly in the Year of the Swap (when Pittsburgh and Philadelphia swapped squads). At 6 feet tall and 186 pounds, No. 37 became one of coach Greasy Neale's building blocks for the Eagles' juggernaut of the future. By the time that juggernaut set sail in 1947, Ernie Steele was a chiseled veteran. Only one other guy on the Birds' 36-man roster had logged more games as an Eagle. And when the '48 squad won the town's first-ever championship, Ernie Steele turned in the one of the key plays of the game—heroics that history seems to have forgotten.

HOW WELL DO YOU KNOW YOUR BIRDS?

The 1948 champion Philadelphia Eagles had a guy on their roster who had once been a member of one of these fabled collegiate units. Which unit was it?

a) The Four Horsemen
b) Mr. Inside and Mr. Outside Backfield
c) Pony Express Backfield
d) Seven Blocks of Granite
e) Galloping Ghostbusters
f) Mighty Mites

MEET ERNIE STEELE

Ernie Steele was born in the little town of Bothell in the state of Washington on November 2, 1917. He grew up in Washington and played football at Highline High School in Seattle. When it came time for college, Ernie explains how he made his choice: "I was going to take a scholarship from Washington State. Before I left, I told them I wasn't going to leave unless they gave my fiancée, Jo, a scholarship too. They didn't do it, so I decided to become a Washington Husky."

Ernie starred as halfback for the Huskies from 1939 to 1941. In one memorable college game in 1940 against archrival Washington State, he scored on 87-yard kickoff and 83-yard punt returns. After college, he was working on the Seattle docks when an old Washington teammate, Jack Stackpool, called him and told him to come to Philly. "Jack said they were looking for a running back and he told them, 'I got just the guy for you!'" Ernie recalls. "So Jo and I—yes, the two of us got married, and we've been married 65 years now—took every penny we could scrape up and hauled off to Philadelphia. Best move I ever made in my life. You know, on the 60th anniversary of the Steagles, I was invited back to Pittsburgh. They were honoring us. There were only six of us left. And then recently, my health hasn't been so good. Mr. Rooney out in Pittsburgh heard about me not feeling so good and he sent me a Steelers' T-shirt. How about that?

"I played as a rookie for Philadelphia because the year I joined the NFL, Pittsburgh and Philadelphia swapped teams. So I played my first year with Philadelphia. I played the next season with the Steagles. Then I played with the Eagles the rest of the way, all the way up to that first championship in the blizzard. Then I quit. I owned a restaurant back in Seattle, and I decided it was time to go back and run it full time and raise my family. We had twin daughters in 1947. The Eagles didn't want me to quit, though, and I still have a telegram from the Rams to come down and see them after I had quit. Not only that, I was on my way to doing something else athletically in '48. I was ready to compete in the 1948 Olympics with the U.S. bobsled team, but then my partner was injured in an accident and I had to give up on that little dream.

After 1948, Ernie threw himself full-time into his eponymous restaurant, Ernie Steele's, in the Capitol Hill neighborhood of Seattle. Over the next half-century, he became a Seattle icon there, much like ex-Phillies great Lefty O'Doull and his tavern did in San Francisco. (Lefty still holds the Phils' all-time modern record for highest single-season batting average.) Ernie was considered quite a character. His 1940s-esque restaurant lasted till 1993, virtually unchanged since the '40s. In '93, he sold Ernie Steele's and the restaurant was renamed Ileen's.

To show the kind of guy Ernie was, here's how he describes the time he ran for sheriff of King County. "I voted for my opponent," Ernie chuckles. "I don't know why I did that. 'Cause we were good friends, I guess." Ernie lost the election (presumably by more than one vote).

BUILDING UP TO THE GAME

The 1947 Eagles wowed an understandably skeptical city. The Eagles team had been perennial cellar-dwellers. That mode fit snugly into the city's athletic performance. For modern-day fans who rue the curse of Billy Penn, consider the plight of Phillysport in the '40s.

From 1940 to 1947, the Phillies finished dead last in all but two seasons. In 1948, they "blasted all the way up to sixth." The city rejoiced. It wasn't a Bronx cheer. There was reason to rejoice. The Phillies' Bob Carpenter-ownership era had infused the team with quality players like Del Ennis, Richie Ashburn, Granny Hamner, Dick Sisler, Robin Roberts, and Curt Simmons—the backbone of the team that was to win a pennant three seasons later. Meanwhile, the Philadelphia Athletics mirrored the Phils' woes or, more accurately, woefulness. From 1940-1946, the A's managed to climb out of the American League basement only once. Then suddenly, in 1947, they jetted up to fifth place. In 1948, they ascended into the first division for the first time since 1933, posting a glitzy 84-70, their best winning percentage since a 94-60 second-place 1932 finish.

Then there were the Eagles. Our Iggles were hardly the toast of the town in the '30s, when they failed to produce even a single winning season. In seven campaigns that decade, they won more than three games only twice. They limped into the '40s with seasons of 1-10, 2-8-1, and 2-9 before topping .500 for the first time as the Steagles. In 1944, the Eagles finally took flight, placing second in each of the next three seasons.

The 1947 edition of the Birds took the division crown and then came oh-so-close to winning it all. They ended up on the losing end of a 28-21 score to the powerhouse Chicago Cardinals, who had also been a perennially horrendous team. The Cards forever played weak sister to the cross-town Windy-City darlings—the Chicago Bears, George Halas'

Monsters of the Midway. But in 1947, at least, the Cards had assembled a dominating squad and outshined "Da Bears."

The Eagles blew into the 1948 season full of hope and swagger. After the first two weeks of the season, however, members of Philly's fair-weather flock started dropping off the bandwagon faster than volunteers on a Mark Foley congressional page sign-up list. The Cards whipped the Birds in the opener 21-14. Next, the Birds tied the L.A. Rams. From that point on, the Birds were killer. They trounced the Giants and Redskins by identical 45-0 scores and squeaked by the mighty Bears 12-7 in the midst of an eight-game winning streak before losing to Boston 37-21. They closed out the season with a 45-21 butt-kicking of Detroit on December 12, 1948. That victory set the stage for the NFL championship rematch with the Cards the following week.

The Cards did not enter the fray in tip-top condition. Paul Christman, the Cards' precision passer, was not slated to start (and he did not) because of a broken finger on his pitching hand. Still, the Cards had beaten the Eagles five consecutive times prior to the '48 NFL championship match (shades of Tampa Bay before they came to town in 2003, after the Eagles had beaten the Bucs four straight times and seemed to have TB's number). That made the Cardinals 3 ½-point favorites.

The Eagles had clinched their division title a few weeks prior to the end of the season. The Cards, despite posting an 11-1-0 record, did not. They had to win the final game of the season against "Da Bears." In a humanitarian footnote to the Eagles' season, right after they clinched, the Birds voted a share of the championship-game money to Stan Mauldin's widow. Mauldin was a tackle for the Chicago Cardinals who collapsed and died of a brain hemorrhage in the team dressing room during the season. (Mauldin's No. 7 is one of only four Cardinals jerseys retired. The others are Larry Wilson, No. 8, JV Cain, No. 88, and Marshall Goldberg, No. 99.) Since the Western Division race was up for grabs, the Eagles wanted to make sure his wife got the money if the Cards didn't make it to the championship game.

THE GAME OF MY LIFE
DECEMBER 19, 1948

Ernie Steele: "We were happy to play those fellows again and to get them at home. The year before, they beat us in the championship game on a field that was covered with ice. Even so, that game was something to behold. You should have seen all the long touchdowns in that game. [There were seven, and five of them were longer than 44 yards.] We Eagles were a fine group of proud athletes and we relished another shot at the Cards because we didn't think there was any finer team than ours. They had some fine boys on that [Cards] team, especially that backfield of Charley Trippi, Paul Christman, Pat Harder, and Elmer Angsman, but we had Bosh [Pritchard] and Steve Van Buren and a fine passer in Tommy Thompson.

"Everything was set and all of Philadelphia was excited. Then it hit—a huge snowstorm. There was a tarpaulin on the field, but with all the snow piled on it, they couldn't get it off! You should have seen us all out on the field, pulling that huge old thing off. Both teams! They had to put flags and stakes on the field so the referees could tell where the yard markers and end zone were. They didn't even measure for first downs in that game. The ref's decision [Ronald Gibbs officiated the game] was final, and that's the way we all had to accept it.

"You know those Philly fans, though, they showed up anyway! The football commissioner was going to call the game, but he didn't. And the game went on and lots of fans showed up. Fact is, we couldn't see the fans. We couldn't see anything! There were only a couple of passes thrown the whole game [there were five passing attempts] and one of them was a long one [65 yards] to our end, Jack Ferante. But guess what? We were offside and it went for naught!

"In conditions like that, we dominated the game. We just couldn't take the ball in. But they didn't seem to be able to move at all. [Ernie is correct: Chicago only got past the Eagles' 30 one time. When that drive sputtered to a halt, the Cardinals' Pat Harder missed a 37-yard field goal try.]

"Nobody scored in the first half. It was gonna be awful tough to score in that blizzard. Then Chicago fumbled and we got it. [Chicago's QB, Ray Mallouf, coughed it up and Bucko Kilroy recovered for the Eagles on the Cardinals' 17.] We ran a couple of plays, as I recall, and then the quarter ended and we had to trudge all the way down the field through that snow. Then we really fooled the Cards, I think. We ran Bosh Pritchard and then Joe Muha, when all the while they were looking out for Van Buren. We ground out a first down without having Van Buren lug it once, but once we were set up inside the 10, Tommy Thompson handed the ball to Van Buren. Steve slammed through a big hole that Vic Sears opened up and lugged it right in.

"Well, I don't want to brag, but near the end of the game, I made the biggest play I ever made. The Cardinals were threatening, but then they tossed out a pass that I intercepted [at the Eagles' 15]. Turns out that was the last play of my career! We got the ball and just hammered down the field with Steve Van Buren. We surprised them a few times on the drive with some quarterback sneaks. Tommy Thompson was a great passer, but he wasn't much for carrying the ball. Anyway, when the game ended, we were inside their 5-yard line and Philadelphia had its first championship."

WRAP

The 1948 championship game brought Philadelphia a second NFL championship. The Frankford Yellow Jackets had won the first title in 1926. The '48 championship game also marked the end of Ernie Steele's stellar career, in which he scored 19 touchdowns, rushed for 1,337 yards, caught 31 passes, returned 94 punts and kickoffs, made 13 fumble recoveries, and intercepted 24 passes. He led all Eagles in interceptions in the '40s, but none of those interceptions were as big as the one he made in that Philadelphia blizzard on December 19, 1948.

"HOW WELL DO YOU KNOW YOUR BIRDS?" ANSWER
d) Seven Blocks of Granite (Center/linebacker and future NFL Hall of Famer Alex Wojciechowicz was a member of Fordham's legendary unit, whose ranks included Green Bay coach Vince Lombardi and five others who, as college textbooks say, "will be left to the student to research"—but if/when you do, you have an unbeatable bar bet.)

Chapter 2

VIC SEARS

"SO, WHAT WAS THE GAME OF YOUR LIFE?"

Vic Sears: "I can think of the game of my life right away, but before I tell you, I've got to mention some other wonderful games and some other wonderful memories I had as a Philadelphia Eagle. First, there was that unusual season when we were the Steagles. Naturally, that was memorable to me. Here I was, a young man from the West Coast, all the way out on the East Coast and playing for a team that was just thrown together for one season because of the war. I can't say it went real smooth. The two head coaches really didn't get along. The Steelers had Walt Kiesling and the Eagles had Greasy Neale. They were always at each other. I was only a young player at that point with only a couple of big-league years under my belt. I thought maybe that's just the way it was up here. Eventually, the owners stepped in and tried to make peace. They made Greasy head of the offense and Kiesling head of the defense. It seems like that's the way all the teams do it nowadays, but that was uncommon in those days. I saw it my rookie year on the Steagles and never again in all the years I played.

"Of course, I was involved in a little bit of controversy myself. You know, all the fellows that had starting jobs with the Steelers and the Eagles had to compete with each other for that job when they joined the two teams together as the Steagles. Well, the Steelers had a pretty good ol' fellow, Eberle Schultz, who started at tackle for them. And then I came along, and you know what? I won that starting job, and I don't think Mr. Schultz was too happy about the arrangement. But I started that Steagles season—the only season the Steagles ever existed—and I was picked as an All-Pro that year. Imagine that! And it was also the first winning season the Eagles ever had—even if they had to pair up with Pittsburgh to achieve it! So every game that year was memorable to a big ol' country boy from Oregon.

"I'd say my string of memorable games started in 1947. That's when the Eagles—the Philadelphia Eagles—really started to excel. Boy, did the city love us in those days! Our opening game that season was a wild one! We beat Washington 45-42 at that huge Philly stadium. I think they tore it down now. [Vic is referring to Philadelphia's now-departed Municipal Stadium.] The Redskins had Sammy Baugh, and let me tell you, if there was ever a finer passer, I don't know who it would be. But we beat the Redskins, and you know what? At the time, that was the most points ever scored in an NFL game. Tommy Thompson, our quarterback, was terrific too. [Thompson threw three TD passes in that game.] And Steve Van Buren hauled a punt in and ran it all the way back—a thing of beauty.

"Then later that season—actually, after the regular season—on a bitter, cold Pennsylvania day, we played the Steelers in a playoff game. That was a thrill for me, seeing as how I had been drafted by Pittsburgh and then played for the Steagles. Funny, huh? That was a thrill, that game—first time the Eagles ever played in a championship-type game. I put it that way because it wasn't actually a championship game, just a playoff for the championship game. So I happened to be fortunate enough to be there for lots of historical firsts for the Eagles. As for that Pittsburgh playoff game, that day was just wonderful. We played a really good game. I remember in this game, Bosh Pritchard—boy, that little man knew how to carry a football!—ran a punt back for a touchdown. And our defense, we just stopped Pittsburgh cold. What a day!

"But OK, you asked me for my most memorable game, so now I'll tell you. It was the championship game against the Los Angeles Rams. We played in a pouring rain. Growing up in Oregon, I was used to rain, but let me tell you, it rained cats and dogs that day! And Steve Van Buren ran all over the field. I think he set a record that day. But the most important reason I picked that as the game of my life is that I got married 10 days before the game! I stayed married to that wonderful woman the rest of my life. A wonderful woman and a second NFL championship—I was on top of the world."

Vic Sears came east from Oregon State to become one of the chief building blocks of the Philadelphia Eagles dynasty in the late '40s. The 6-foot-3, 226-pound athlete was one of Philly's unsung gridiron heroes of that era. Sears was an All-Pro tackle as a Phil-Pitt "Steagle" and again in 1949 with the championship Philadelphia Eagles. History remembers No. 79 as one of the premiere linemen of the '40s. He retired in 1953, having spent his entire NFL career as an Eagle.

HOW WELL DO YOU KNOW YOUR BIRDS?

In 1943, the Philadelphia Eagles and Pittsburgh Steelers combined into one team, Phil-Pitt or Pitt-Phil, that was known popularly as the "Steagles," although that particular name was never sanctioned by the NFL. In 1944, the Philadelphia contingent re-formed as the Philadelphia Eagles. However, the Pittsburgh Steelers couldn't shake the habit. They combined forces once more with another NFL team. What team did Pittsburgh combine with in the 1944 campaign?

a) Chicago Bears
b) Washington Redskins
c) Canton Bulldogs
d) Cincinnati Bengals
e) Detroit Lions
f) Chicago Cardinals
g) St. Louis Cardinal
h) Cleveland Browns

MEET VIC SEARS

Born March 4, 1918, Victor Wilson Sears grew up in Eugene, Oregon, in the '20s and '30s. He attended school in a one-room schoolhouse with 15 other classmates, all of different ages. As Vic recalls, "I never even saw a football game. I didn't know a thing about the sport till I was 15. That's when I was a high school sophomore. My older brother played football. That made me want to play, too, so I joined the team. I didn't have a uniform that fit, so I made my own! Can you imagine one of these fellas today doing that? I was an ol' farm boy, though. We all knew how to use those old Singer sewing machines. I wore my uniform the next day at practice. The coach saw me and told me to tackle this other boy. I whacked the guy pretty good and it really shocked the coach. I was a tall, gangly kid at the time and I could tell the coach didn't expect me to be able to sock somebody as hard as I did. I know I made an impression on the coach. Next day, he gave me sneakers, pants—everything. I got to be a pretty good player and wound up getting a football scholarship to Oregon State. I majored in health education."

Vic Sears was the fourth man picked in the 1941 draft. "You want to know how Greasy Neale came to know about me?" Vic Sears chuckles. "A newspaper reporter for the *Portland Oregonian* tipped him off that I was a pretty fair country player. So I got to Pittsburgh—that's who drafted me—and Greasy looked at me. So did that playboy owner they had at the time, Lex Thompson, who had just bought the Steelers. And I think they were both disappointed. They had a different notion of what a tackle should look like! You see, Greasy was a tough ol' bird. He had played with Jim Thorpe, and to Greasy, a tackle was supposed to be a mean-lookin' cuss. I was baby-faced and rangy."

But Vic impressed the football establishment and won the starting tackle job for the Eagles. How did that happen when the Steelers drafted and never traded him? Hang on, football fans. These were wild and wooly times in the NFL, so here's a strange tale of two cities, NFL style.

In 1940, Pittsburgh Steelers owner Art Rooney sold his team to Alexis Thompson of New York. Lex was a mere 30 years old at the time and heir to a fortune of six million dollars in steel stocks. The following year, Bert Bell, the original Eagles owner—who was now half-owner of the Eagles with longtime friend Art Rooney—swapped franchises with Lex Thompson. Yes, the Steelers came to Philly and the Eagles went to Pittsburgh. (Too bad they didn't defer the swap till the mid-'70s.) So, via a bizarre twist, Steelers draftee Vic Sears found himself donning Eagle green his first season. Shaking his head, Vic says, "No, actually, in those days, our Eagles uniforms were black and gray or maybe black and silver." (Black and silver? Were our '40s Eagles the inspiration for Raider Nation?)

The transplanted Steelers did no better than their Eagles precursors. (The 1941 Birds were 2-8-1, while the '42 edition was 2-9, so the Eagles actually slipped from fourth to fifth place after the swap.) As for the tale of two cities, it continued. The following year, the Eagles and Steelers combined forces and fashioned a 5-4-1 record.

"A very nice fellow who used to be a reporter for Public Radio [Matthew Algeo] talked to me a while back," Vic recounts. "He wrote a wonderful book [*Last Team Standing: How the Steelers and the Eagles—The Steagles—Saved Pro Football During World War II*] about our Steagles team that year. This young man ... figured that the NFL might have folded after the war if they had stopped NFL football. They didn't have enough young men to field a roster for all the teams because they were off fighting the war. By combining the Eagles and Steelers, they cut down on the number of overall NFL roster slots and the league could go on.

"As for the competition—well see, when that other league, the AAFC, the league the Cleveland Browns were in, came along after the war, according to this fellow, the NFL might not have been well enough established if they had folded during the war to fight off their competition. Who knows? I'll tell you, there were certainly some fine boys playing in that other league.

"We Steagles played our home games in two different cities. We wound up playing four games at the old Shibe Park in Philly and two games at Forbes Field in Pittsburgh. Anyway, I was proud because it was the first Eagles team—even if it wasn't *really* an Eagles team—that ever had a winning record, at least up to that point. After that year [1943], we got Steve Van Buren and we started getting good.

"The '40s were a wonderful time for me because of all the fine boys I met with the Eagles. Greasy used to tell us, 'We don't make much money, but we sure have fun.' He was right. We certainly didn't get paid very much, but what a wonderful time I had in Philadelphia. Things turned around in the '50s. We started to slip and by 1953, I was too worn down to keep playing. But they certainly were wonderful times."

BUILDING UP TO THE GAME

The team entered the 1949 season on the heels of besting the Chicago Cardinals 7-0 in a Philly blizzard that saw the Eagles crowned as NFL champs for the first time. In front of 4,355 New York fans, the Birds kicked off their campaign with a measly 7-0 victory over the NY Bulldogs. Philadelphia followed with a win over Detroit and an emotional 28-3 thumping of the Chicago Cardinals in a rematch of the '48 championship tilt. "We may have used up all our emotion in that Cardinals game," Vic says, reflecting on the season. "We wanted to prove the blizzard win was no fluke." Perhaps Vic is right. The following week, the Bears handed the Birds their only loss in the '49 campaign.

The Eagles steamrolled the opposition the rest of the way. The closest any opponent came to them was 14 points—in a game the Eagles convincingly won 17-3 over the Giants. Vic Sears explains the anatomy of the powerhouse: "We were basically a running team. We had Van Buren, but we also had Bosh Pritchard, who didn't get the credit he deserved. We also had swell receivers like Jack Ferrante, who never went to college, and Pete Pihos. And we had a defense like nobody's business."

So the defending champs, the Philadelphia Eagles, flew west to try to batter the Los Angeles Rams in the NFL title game. As Vic said, "We couldn't wait for that championship money! We got $766 in 1947 when we lost to the Cardinals in the championship game. Next year, when we won that championship game in the blizzard, each of us got $1,540 for the winner's share. That was big money in those days, and we were all excited about the prospects of a big payoff."

THE GAME OF MY LIFE
DECEMBER 18, 1949

Vic Sears: "It was a thrill for me to get back to the West Coast. I had played in Los Angeles as a college boy. I played against Jackie Robinson when he was with UCLA. What a great runner he was! But I figured him out. I could tell which way he was going by the way he planted his feet.

"I was happy to be going back to warmer weather. I remember that cold weather—the blizzard—in the championship game the year before. And we were going to play the game in the Coliseum. What an impressive place that was. It was built long ago [in 1922] but it seemed pretty new [in 1949]. They held the Olympics there. Anyway, our whole team was thrilled about playing there.

"Those Rams were a talented team. They were the first ones in football to put an insignia on their helmets. Just a couple years earlier, in about '47 or '48, as I recall, the Rams painted ram horns on their helmets. [Actually, a Rams HB named Fred Gehrke allegedly painted horns on the Rams' helmets—the term "butthead" hadn't yet entered the vernacular. Yes, *Back to the Future* fans, Biff was using an anachronism.]

"We got out to that field and it was pouring rain. That's something, isn't it? Southern California and we run into a torrential rain. It was the second year in a row we played a championship game in terrible conditions and it was the second year in a row that we ended up shutting out the opponent. They tell me no other team has ever done that. Nobody else has ever won two consecutive NFL championships by shutout. Of course, this was a real special trip for me, returning to the West Coast with my new wife for the first time. That made everything extra special.

"What a game! Steve Van Buren … I don't think I ever saw Steve play better, and that's saying something. He ran all over the field. [Van Buren gained 197 yards.] We only scored two TDs all day. The first came on a pass from Tommy Thompson, our one-eyed quarterback, to Pete Pihos. I felt good about that because I hung in there in that slippery field and gave Tommy time to find that receiver. … And Pete Pihos—what a tough guy! He played at Indiana and never missed a game for us. Pete was one of the best players I ever saw on both offense and defense. Everybody knows Chuck Bednarik as a great two-way player, but they forget about Pete.

"Then we scored again when Leo Skladany blocked a Bob Waterfield punt and then fell on it for a score. That was it. It was all we needed. We beat the Rams 14-0. You know, speaking about that Bob Waterfield, he had a terrific arm, too. He was one of the greatest quarterbacks I played against and he was a real Hollywood type, too. He was married to Jane Russell, who was one of the biggest names in Hollywood. Well, we got the best of the Hollywood boys that day.

"The Eagles were really good to me. Next year at training camp in Two Rivers, Wisconsin, the Eagles sent me and my bride tickets to come to camp. We took them up on it. We had honeymooned with my parents on their farm in Oregon and then we went to camp. I was glad I did because that was the last year we were allowed to bring wives to camp. Those old-timers believed in that 'wilderness' thing.

"As for the Eagles, after that '49 championship our fortunes changed, but that championship … I'll never forget that day! I was with the woman that I was going to spend the rest of my life with, and I had just earned what turned out to be the last championship check I would ever receive."

WRAP

The future looked rosy for the Iggles. Philadelphia was the toast of the NFL. Meanwhile, over in the All-American Football Conference, the Cleveland Browns won their fourth consecutive title, defeating the San Francisco 49ers 21-7. Essentially, the Browns' domination did in the league. The AAFC folded after the '49 season, and some AAFC teams, including the Browns, jumped to the NFL. Paul Brown, the outspoken, anything-but-humble coach of the Cleveland Browns, was proclaiming the superiority of his team. The schedulers pitted the AAFC-champ Cleveland Browns against the NFL-champ Philadelphia Eagles in the 1950 season opener. The football world awaited an onslaught. And it happened—just not the way it was predicted. The Browns trounced the Eagles 35-10. Unfortunately, that game ushered in a decade-long Eagles demise. By 1956, the team had dropped down to last place.

"HOW WELL DO YOU KNOW YOUR BIRDS?" ANSWER
f) The Chicago Cardinals (And they went 0-11. After that season, the Steelers and the Cardinals went their separate ways for good. Pittsburgh has remained forever in the Steel City—Pittsburgh doesn't seem to appreciate being called the Smoky City anymore—while the Cardinals flew off to St. Louis and then to Arizona.)

Chapter 3

TOMMY McDONALD

"SO, WHAT WAS THE GAME OF YOUR LIFE?"

Tommy McDonald: "I know you're going to be talking to a few guys from our '60 team for this book. I gotta tell you Bob, I loved that book you wrote about our '60 team. For all of us on that team, the championship game is the game that immediately pops into our heads whenever we go down memory lane. That's the season we all remember best. The guys on the '60 team come from a different era in so many ways. I believe we might have gotten more out of the game back then. Teams seemed to be closer-knit in those days. So when you ask one of us what the game of our life was, I tend to think about big team wins. Looking at it that way, what game could possibly be more important than the championship game at Franklin Field in 1960? But if I think of a great game based on my personal performance, it would be our game against the Giants in 1959. I played that game with a broken jaw. My jaw was wired shut! I caught three TD passes and ran a punt back 81 yards for another score. So yeah, the championship game sticks out for me— same as it does for every other member of that '60 squad—but the next game that really sticks out would have to be that '59 game against New York."

Tommy McDonald was an All-American on Bud Wilkinson's undefeated Oklahoma juggernaut of the '50s. Tommy was the biggest name on the Sooners squad and perhaps the biggest collegiate football name in the nation. That's nothing to sneeze at. In a draft class that boasted Jimmy Brown, Sonny Jurgensen, Jack Pardee, Henry Jordan, Jim Parker, and Jon Arnett, Tommy McDonald emerged as the Maxwell Club Award winner as college football's best player. Nonetheless, because of his diminutive stature, Tommy wasn't drafted till the third round of the 1957 NFL draft. Philadelphia's "gamble" paid off. Tommy McDonald ended his Hall of Fame career as a six-time Pro Bowler who averaged 17 yards per catch and tallied 84 career TDs.

HOW WELL DO YOU KNOW YOUR BIRDS?

Which of these former Eagles did not win the Maxwell Award as the nation's top collegiate football player?

a) Chuck Bednarik   b) Davey O'Brien
c) Pete Pihos   d) Ty Detmer
e) Tommy McDonald

MEET TOMMY McDONALD

Thomas Franklin McDonald was born in Roy, New Mexico, on July 26, 1934. "My biggest break was moving to Albuquerque for my last two years in high school. Roy was such a small town. If our family had stayed in Roy, I would never have been noticed or discovered. I'll tell you how small Roy was [and still is]. A few years ago, I was asked to come back and speak at the high school graduation in Roy. You know how many graduates they had? Seven! So for me, moving to Albuquerque was a blessing from the big guy upstairs. I had a chance for people to see my God-given talent once I got to Albuquerque."

As a high schooler, McDonald excelled in basketball, track, and football under the tutelage of Hugh Hackett, who coached him in football and track. In his senior year at Highland High School in Albuquerque, Tommy won five gold medals in the state track finals. He also set a New Mexico high school basketball record by scoring 595 points in a single season. "I got scholarship offers from all kinds of schools—SMU, Texas, TCU, and others—but I liked Oklahoma best for one reason. Oklahoma's coach, [Bud] Wilkinson, told me, 'Tommy, if the only reason you're coming here is to play football, I don't want you. Right now, the most important thing for you personally is to get an education.' That impressed me. I thought, 'No other coach has ever said those words to me.' Mr. Wilkinson acted like he took a personal interest in me. Once I played football for him, I found out he really did care about me personally."

In his collegiate years, Tommy churned up the turf as a running back. As a Sooner, he developed a lifelong knack for finding his way to pay dirt whenever he got his hands on the pigskin. In 1955, he became the first Sooner ever to score a touchdown in every game in a season. In fact, during his junior and senior years, he scored a TD in 20 out of 21 games. Tommy was a running back in Oklahoma's split-T offense. He was a double threat who could not only run the ball, but also throw it pretty accurately. His greatest talent, catching a football—the skill that would eventually land him a spot in Canton, Ohio—lay dormant and virtually untapped at Oklahoma. In Bud Wilkinson's successful, run-intensive offense, Tommy hardly ever cruised under an aerial.

As fate would have it, Tommy was inserted into the Eagles offense as a wide receiver after a few games in his rookie season. He was never removed from that role—a role he was born to play.

Truth be told, inserting Tommy into the Philadelphia starting lineup as flanker did not prove a panacea for the low-flying Birds of the mid- to late '50s. Philadelphia still managed to finish dead last in '58, despite the presence of Tommy and former L.A. Rams quarterback Norm Van Brocklin, who joined the Eagles flock that year. Nonetheless, as the Van Brocklin-led Birds continued to gain proficiency and confidence in the pass-oriented system their feisty quarterback preached, they rose in the standings. In '59, they tied for second place.

The following year, the mighty Eagles soared to heights long before John Ashcroft sang about soaring eagles or spruced up constitutions. "We won the championship that year, but you know, Bob," Tommy McDonald reminisces, "unfortunately, another game I remember all too well is the opening-day loss to Cleveland in '60. We got thumped 41-24. That game really shook me up. It shook all of us up. After we finished second in '59, we thought we'd be bona fide contenders in 1960. The way Jimmy Brown and Bobby Mitchell ran all over Franklin Field that day, I know the fans were really wondering how good their Eagles really were.

"That opening-day loss was a tough one, a character test for the whole team. Fortunately, we ran off nine straight wins afterwards. When I look back now, we actually won our division pretty easily considering the talent the Giants and the Browns had."

In the 1960 NFL championship tilt, Tommy McDonald scored the first of the Birds' two TDs to help Philadelphia win its last NFL championship. After that 1960 high, however, it was virtually all downhill for Eagles football.

The Eagles managed a second-place finish in 1961. McDonald had a great season with new QB and future Hall of Famer Sonny Jurgensen tossing him the ball. "Jurgensen to McDonald" became Philadelphia's most famous sporting cry, rivaled at the time only by "Dipper Dunk" and "Gola Goal." The QB-flanker duo even hosted their own TV show at the height of their popularity. Unfortunately, after finishing second in 1961, the Eagles plummeted. In 1964, Joe Kuharich came to town and traded away both Jurgensen and McDonald. Tommy went to the Rams, followed by stints in Dallas, Atlanta, and Cleveland, where he finished his career in 1968. Indisputably, however, the greatest performances in McDonald's distinguished career came while wearing a Philadelphia Eagles uniform (No. 25, as all of Philly knew).

"I have to tell you a funny story about what happened when I came to Philly," Tommy laughs. "Philly didn't exactly roll out the red carpet for me! I drove into town and I wasn't quite sure where I was going. I stopped at a store to ask for directions. Then, when I left the store, the woman I had spoken with called the cops. It seems there was a cat burglar running around loose that the police had been looking for, and unfortunately for me, I fit the guy's description. [Evidently he was very handsome—right, Tommy?] So they hauled me into the police station. I didn't know anyone in Philadelphia except Vince McNally [the Eagles' owner at the time], so I called him. Fortunately, he came down to the station and straightened the whole thing out! But once I got past that rocky start, I've lived in Philadelphia ever since. Philadelphia has been a wonderful place for my family and me."

BUILDING UP TO THE GAME

"In my rookie year of 1957, I started the season out sitting on the bench for the most part," Tommy recollects. "I had never sat on the bench in my life. It was really tough on me. I ran back kickoffs and punts, but didn't get into the game too often for scrimmage plays."

No one really knew what to expect of Tommy McDonald as a rookie. He had enjoyed a storybook collegiate career that culminated in his winning Philadelphia's prestigious Maxwell Club Award, yet Tommy was considered a risky investment because the footballerati dismissed him as too small for the pro game.

During McDonald's rookie year in the NFL, New York, Cleveland, and Baltimore seemed to be the franchises headed for glory. The Giants were forging a reputation as the toughest defense in all of pro football, while Jimmy Brown of the Browns was reinventing the running back position. Under Johnny Unitas, the Baltimore Colts were exploring the potentials of the modern pro passing game, cultivating the new tight end position with Raymond Berry and popularizing the long bomb with Penn State's Lenny Moore.

Meanwhile, in the Quaker City, both the Eagles and the Phils had sat atop their respective sports at the beginning of the '50s. The Phils' Whiz Kids exhilarated the city by winning an NL pennant in 1950, while the Eagles copped back-to-back NFL crowns in '48 and '49. As the decade rolled along, however, the fortunes of both declined. As the late '50s unfurled, both the Phils and Eagles became doormats, reprising the roles each had perfected from the late '30s through the mid '40s.

The Iggles were pinning their hopes of resurrection on Norm Van Brocklin, a grizzled veteran leader whose disenchantment with the L.A. Rams led to his exodus. Van Brocklin held a minority opinion. He was convinced that Philadelphia's squad possessed enough football talent to challenge the Giants, the Browns, and the Colts.

Van Brocklin's arrival did not halt the Eagles' skid immediately. The Birds dropped Van Brocklin's first game, the '58 opener, 24-14 to the Redskins. No longer buried deep on the running back chart, second-year man Tommy McDonald was part of his corps of receivers. McDonald had earned a starting receiving slot midway through his rookie season. How? "Our receiver, Bill Stribling, went down with an injury in '57, and I got an unexpected chance—one that turned my career around." Tommy reveals. "Charley Gauer, our coach, sent me in as a receiver to replace Stribling. I had never played or even practiced at that position, but I was happy to get in the game and get a chance."

Gauer didn't select McDonald for the receiving role on a whim. Tommy points out, "I caught four TD passes in college on one play that was in our playbook but we only ran occasionally. Our QB, Jim Harris, would fake the ball to me. I'd go into the line and then cut downfield. Jim would roll out right and look for me deep. Well, Charlie saw that play on a tape of me that the Eagles had looked at. Charley must have had that play somewhere in the back of his mind, 'cause like I said, I was listed as a running back."

Inserted as a receiver, Tommy McDonald remained in the lineup for good. The mighty mite was renowned for his penchant to pop back up on his feet, jack-in-the-box style, as soon as he was upended—usually by opponents often literally double his size. That kind of pluck made the diminutive Tommy McDonald arguably as "big" a fan favorite as Philly ever had. After his conversion to flanker back, Tommy McDonald teamed with Pete Retzlaff and Bobby Walston to form what was arguably the best receiving triumvirate the Quaker City ever cheered. The names of all three of these all-time Eagles stars continue to pepper the Eagles' record book.

"I did well right from the start as a receiver," Tommy recalls. "Of course, all I wanted to do was play and contribute. My rookie season, our starting quarterback was Bobby Thomason. Sonny Jurgensen saw some action too, but Sonny was just a rookie. In my second season, Dutch [Van Brocklin's nickname was 'Dutch' or the 'Dutchman'] arrived on the scene. That guy could toss a football like no one I've ever seen! Dutch kind of floated the ball out to you. All you had to do was to reach out and bring it in. The guy always put the ball in an area where it was easy to reach.

"So by 1959, with guys like Dutch and Sonny throwing to me, I had gained some respect as a receiver. The Eagles were gaining some respect, too. That leads me to that Giants game in '59—the game of my life [besides the '60 championship game]. I broke my jaw against San Francisco in the '59 opener. I was knocked unconscious. You know, I don't think I regained consciousness till I was on the plane flying back to Philly. I can't even remember being in the locker room after the game. I have no recollection of anything that happened from the time I was hit till I came to on the plane. As it turned out, my jaw was broken and they had to wire it shut.

"Sometime that week after I had broken my jaw, the owner of the Eagles, Mr. Vince McNally, came to see me and told me, 'Tommy, you gotta play this Sunday. I know your jaw is broken, but that shouldn't stop you from being able to catch a football. We don't have anybody else we can stick in there in your place.' I didn't know any different! When Mr. McNally said I had to play whether I had a broken jaw or not, I just figured I had no choice. I had to play."

And that's how Tommy McDonald entered Franklin Field on October 4, 1959—a broken-jawed warrior doing the job his boss paid him to do.

As for the contest itself, October 4, 1959, marked the 51st meeting between the Giants and Eagles. The Giants had the better of the overall series, 32-17. Interestingly enough, the woeful Eagles squad of 1958 had bested the mighty Giants in the two teams' last regular-season meeting. As for the two-week-old 1959 season, both Philadelphia and New York had opened their campaigns on the west coast. Both had lost. Still, despite appearing outmanned on paper, the Eagles were hardly intimidated by the New Yorkers. In fact, they topped the Giants 21-17 in the preseason tune-up.

The Eagles had to face the Giants with their forces seriously depleted. Dick Bielski, Ken McAfee, Pete Retzlaff, J.D. Smith, and linebacker Darrell Aschberger were all scratched from the lineup. New York's only missing starter was running back Alex Webster.

THE GAME OF MY LIFE
OCTOBER 4, 1959

Tommy McDonald: "It was one of those hot, Philadelphia, Indian-summer days. The temperature was probably in the 80s. It was one of those games where things just seemed to go our way. We got things going fast on offense. Our first score was a [33-yard] TD pass from Dutch to me after a long drive. [Actually, it was a five-play drive that culminated with a 33-yard scoring strike to McDonald.] I don't think we ever gave up the lead after that.

"Anyway, it wasn't too long after that first touchdown that Van Brocklin threw me another perfect pass—the way only Dutch could throw them. It was a deep pass [55 yards] that I ran under. I got behind—I think it was Lindon Crow—one of their talented defensive backs. When the Giants got the ball, I think they stalled again. They punted and I ran it back 81 yards for a touchdown. I joke with Vai Sikahema about that punt return now. You know, Vai tied me for the Eagles record for longest punt return. 'Cause remember, after Vai returned his punt for a score, he ran over to the goalpost and punched it like a boxer punching a heavy bag. As for my punt return, I remember that Art Powell threw me a great block that sprung me. Bob Pellegrini also wiped out their punter, Don Chandler, and between the two of them, they gave me everything I needed.

"We ended the half with a 21-7 lead and I had scored all three TDs. That was pretty exciting.

"When the second half started, the Giants kicked off to us. Art Powell received it and ran it back 95 yards before he tripped and fell on about the 3-yard line. I never checked this out, but I bet Art's return was the longest return ever that didn't go for a TD. Anyway, a few plays later the Dutchman sneaked one over and we went ahead 28-7.

"As I said, this was one game that seemed to go our way from start to finish. After Dutch scored on the sneak after Art's return, we had another long drive and one of our backs scored on a short dive play. [Theron Sapp scored from 1 yard out.] Then the Giants got the ball and somebody knocked the ball out of [QB Charlie] Connerly's hand, and Chuck Weber, our middle linebacker, recovered in the end zone for another score.

"That wasn't the end. I had one more touchdown. We had recovered a Giants fumble on their 19-yard line and we put Sonny Jurgensen in for Dutch. When Dutch had enough in a game, he used to tell Buck Shaw, our coach, to 'put the kid in.' Sonny was the 'kid.' Anyway, Sonny found me free in the end zone and he hit me for my third TD of the day. So, after three TD catches and an Eagles-record punt return all on the same day, who wouldn't remember a game like that?"

WRAP

The Eagles' underdog victory over the mighty Giants that afternoon sparked a surprise season for the Birds that saw them finish second in a tough Eastern Conference. Things did go the Eagles' way that October day. Although the Eagles dominated on the scoreboard, the statistics were fairly close. Both teams gained 223 yards passing. The difference in the game was turnovers. The Giants lost three, the Eagles none. The other difference was Tommy McDonald. The New York papers claimed that

Tommy had run so unfettered because Giants All-Pro safety Jim Patton was not in the lineup. Tommy said that Eagles owner Vince McNally came up with a more interesting postgame suggestion.

"After the game," Tommy chuckles, "Vince McNally came over to me and congratulated me for a great performance. Then he added, 'If this is the way you play with a broken jaw, we've got to break your jaw more often!'"

"HOW WELL DO YOU KNOW YOUR BIRDS?" ANSWER
c) Pete Pihos

Chapter 4

CHUCK WEBER

"SO, WHAT WAS THE GAME OF YOUR LIFE?"

Chuck Weber: "As for my personal biggest thrill, it was certainly the [1960] championship game. What bigger thrill could there be for a guy who was born in Philadelphia and played football at West Chester—West Chester State Teachers College, as it was known back in the day? To play on the team that won Philadelphia's last NFL championship is something I'm really proud of. But as for a great game that I personally played, a game where my performance really contributed to our team's success, I'd have to go back to that Dallas game in 1960—the first time the Dallas Cowboys and Philadelphia Eagles ever squared off. As a personal performance, that was my best and most unforgettable."

Born on March 25 in the year 1930, Charles Fredrick Weber, Jr. grew up in the Philly area and played his collegiate ball at West Chester. Chuck was the middle linebacker for the 1960 NFL champion Eagles. Although he made Little All-American at offensive guard and was selected as his team's Most Outstanding Player, he was not drafted into the NFL after college. The 6-foot-1, 229-pound athlete joined the Marines after school and played football in the service. After the service, he tried out for the Cleveland Browns in 1955 and made the squad. He logged time for the Browns and the Chicago Cardinals before being dealt to the Eagles in 1959. In Philadelphia, he immediately became the starting middle linebacker. Chuck turned in a fine season for the Eagles, who were in the process of rebuilding in '59. The program was successful. The Eagles climbed from the basement all the way up to second place. In the following season, 1960, when the Eagles went to the toppermost of the NFL, Chuck Weber called the defensive signals in the huddle. In 1961, Chuck again started at middle linebacker before calling it quits at season's end. After his playing days, he commenced a longtime career as coach. Chuck coached football at Abington High School, his alma mater, in 1962. Subsequently, he served as defensive coach for the Boston Patriots, the San Diego Chargers, the Cincinnati Bengals, the St. Louis Cardinals, the Cleveland Browns, and the Baltimore Colts.

HOW WELL DO YOU KNOW YOUR BIRDS?

In only one season did two different Eagles defenders intercept three or more passes in a single game in the same year. What was the season? (The defenders are in parentheses.)

a) 1950 (Russ Craft, Joe Sutton)
b) 1960 (Tommy Brookshier, Chuck Weber)
c) 1965 (Jim Nettles, Nate Ramsey)
d) 2005 (Brian Dawkins, Lito Sheppard)
e) 1985 (Roynell Young, Herman Edwards)
f) 1993 (Eric Allen, Seth Joyner)
g) 2000 (Troy Vincent, Bobby Taylor)
h) 1976 (Randy Logan, Frank LeMaster)

MEET CHUCK WEBER

"Back in 1953, I was the first guy who ever represented West Chester in the NCAA National Wrestling Championships," Chuck Weber reports. "My opponent was a guy from Penn State. I was beating him 3-0, but I had pulled my latissimus dorsus muscle in an AAU tournament the week before. Look, I'm not making excuses, but I always thought I could have won the NCAA Championship that year if I had been healthy."

His loss on the mat notwithstanding, Chuck was voted the greatest athlete in the history of West Chester University in 1977. Chuck had starred not only as a grappler, but also as a gridder.

"I wasn't drafted out of West Chester," Chuck explains. "I went into the service and played football. I also coached baseball and wrestling. In the service, I was picked the Most Outstanding Player on the football team.

"I got several offers to try out for NFL teams as a result of that Most Outstanding Player in the service award," Chuck recounts. "One of the offers came from the Cleveland Browns. I had heard that Paul Brown [the Cleveland Browns' coach at the time] gave a fair shot to guys that didn't have a big name from college. When the last cut came with the Browns, I had to report to Brown's office. I sat outside his office and waited while he talked to the guys ahead of me. When my turn came, I passed by his secretary and asked, 'Did the guy ahead of me look sad when he left?' I had no idea what to expect, but the coach told me I had made the squad."

Chuck spent some time with the Browns and then a few years with the Chicago Cardinals before he was dealt to the Eagles in 1959.

"It was great coming home," Chuck recollects. "I landed a starting job in '59 when I came to Philadelphia and I held it for three years. I was fortunate. I was here during Philly's peak years. [In Chuck's three years with Philly, the Eagles posted a glittering 27-11 record.] So my memories are particularly pleasant."

Chuck hung up his cleats and jersey No. 51 after the 1961 season. He coached at Abington High School for a year before engaging in a long career as an NFL coach. When his NFL days ended, he served as mortgage loan officer of the Great American Bank in San Diego from 1986 to 1992. After he left that position, Chuck bade goodbye to the work-a-day world for good. He is now retired in Arizona.

BUILDING UP TO THE GAME

In 1960, Dallas suddenly had two first-year professional football franchises battling for the heart of Texas. The fledgling Dallas Cowboys were the newest franchise in a solidly established National Football League, while the rival Dallas Texans represented Big D in the upstart American Football League. The AFL was premiering that year. At the time, newspapers described Dallas as a "Gate Town," which meant that spectators didn't purchase their tickets until right before the game. Consequently, the vagaries of Texas weather exerted undue influence on gate receipts. In the Cowboys' debut the week prior to the Eagles tilt,

45,000 fans had been expected to show. However, a torrential rain fell the night before the game, and only 30,000 fans spun the turnstiles.

Tom Landry was the Cowboys' coach. Landry had gained considerable renown as the New York Giants offensive coach under head coach Jim Lee Howell in the late '50s. Landry's defensive counterpart on the Giants' coaching staff was Vince Lombardi. Although the Cowboys were not expected to be an impact team—given that their squad was patched together from throw-away players grudgingly made available by each pre-existing NFL team—they had gotten off to a surprisingly strong start against the Pittsburgh Steelers. Although the 'Boys lost the contest, the 35-28 score was amazingly close. Moreover, diminutive Dallas QB Eddie LeBaron, who had starred for years as a Washington Redskin, completed 15 of 28 passes for 345 yards and three TDs.

Ex-Eagle and University of Maryland star Dick Bielski led a capable crop of Cowboys receivers whose litany included Fred Dugan, Jim Doran, Ray Mathews, and Billy Houghton. Houghton had starred for years in the NFL. In fact, he ended his career one notch ahead of Tommy McDonald on the NFL's all-time list both for career catches and total yards receiving.

After losing the opener at home to Cleveland, the Eagles needed a victory to get untracked. The squad showed its resiliency the week before the game. "We had a fine week of practice," coach Buck Shaw was quoted at the time. "Our fellows have shaken off that Cleveland game. We're set to go out and win one this week."

THE GAME OF MY LIFE
SEPTEMBER 30, 1960

Chuck Weber: "There was hardly anyone in the stands that night. It was a night game, you know, and it was hot. [It was a muggy 84 degrees at game time.] In those days, there was hardly any TV coverage, at least compared to nowadays. I think they only broadcast the away games in Philadelphia. We played 12 games a season, and only six of them were broadcast. [Actually, the Dallas game was *not* broadcast on Philadelphia TV.] We played in the Cotton Bowl, and really, in those days, Dallas was a collegiate town. People down there were more interested in college football than the pros.

"You know, Dutch [Eagles QB Norm Van Brocklin] got off to a bad start in the opener. He eventually won the MVP that season and he deserved it, but he threw a few interceptions against Cleveland in the first game and we got trounced. He didn't start off much better in the Dallas game the following week. I think he threw an interception early in the game and Dallas cashed in with a field goal. We came back with some field goals ourselves. [Bobby Walston kicked a pair of FGs as the Eagles took a 6-3 lead.] I think Dallas tied us again, but then Dutch found Tommy McDonald in the end zone. Tommy was wide open, which wasn't unusual. He left the Dallas defender standing there. [Tommy beat ex-Penn Stater Fred Doelling.] Anyway, the score put us ahead 13-6.

"Things looked good because Bobby Freeman, a really underrated player that championship year, intercepted a pass. Our offense drove inside the 10 and then Billy Barnes threw one away to Dallas. Billy Ray used to run a halfback pass play really well, but he didn't this time. Anyway, that interception let Dallas back into the game, and they took full advantage of it and scored. [QB LeBaron hit receiver Frank Clarke with a 75-yard scoring strike.]

"Next thing I know, Bobby Freeman—maybe he was embarrassed 'cause he was the guy that Frank Clarke beat on the TD—broke through and blocked the extra point. So we came out of that whole exchange with a slim one-point lead. ... Billy Barnes ended up scoring a couple of touchdowns on runs, so he redeemed himself for throwing that interception earlier in the game.

"As for myself, I got lucky that day. I don't know if I was reading LeBaron well or what, but I finished the night with three interceptions. It seemed like every time Dallas got a threat going, we'd come up with an interception. ... Dallas didn't win a game all year, and if we had lost to them, we would have started the '60 season 0-2. I don't think we'd have gone all the way if that had happened because New York and Cleveland had such talent on their squads. An 0-2 start would have been too much to overcome. So when you look back on that championship season, the Dallas game turned out to be a key game. It was our first win in a nine-game streak. I'm just proud that I got a chance to play such a big part in the win. It's a game I'll never forget."

WRAP

When the final gun went off, the Eagles had won a squeaker by virtue. The difference in score boiled down to not one, but two blocked point-after-touchdown attempts, both by the Eagles' Bobby Freeman. In reality, the Cowboys probably outplayed the Eagles. However, Chuck Weber's timely interceptions consistently turned the tide whenever Dallas appeared poised to take control of the game. After the game, coach Buck Shaw observed, "That was the longest 60 minutes I ever spent in football. I knew we were a better team, but I was afraid all the way through that we would pull some boners and hand the game to them."

The Birds' defensive line at that point in the 1960 season was hardly championship caliber. Opponents had tallied over 500 yards on the ground in the first two games of the season. However, the pass defense, led that evening by Chuck Weber, had saved the day—and with it, Philadelphia's last championship season.

Chapter 5

CHUCK BEDNARIK

"SO, WHAT WAS THE GAME OF YOUR LIFE?"

Chuck Bednarik: "I played in so many big games with the Eagles. I played in the last two championship games the Eagles ever played in. They were defending champs when I came up as a rookie in 1949. We had a great team in '49. What a defense! We shut the Rams out in the championship game in a pouring rainstorm. No team in NFL history has ever won two straight championships by shutout, but the '48 and '49 Eagles did. I wasn't on the '48 team, but I was on the '49 team, so that championship-game shutout was pretty unforgettable. Then there was the 1960 championship game. In that one, I played both ways, offense and defense. We won a great victory because those Packers that we beat were a great team. All during the years when I grew up, the Packers always seemed to have powerhouse teams. The people, the citizens of Green Bay, really support their team, so it was a thrill to beat those Packers here at Franklin Field, the place I had played in college for Penn. But let me tell you, that whole 1960 season is pretty unforgettable, and the game I remember most that season was our win over the Giants in Yankee Stadium. That was the game I knocked Frank Gifford out. That was some game!"

Ask Philadelphians of any era, "Who is No. 60?" and they'll respond, "Chuck Bednarik." Recognized to this day as the greatest Eagle of them all,

Chuck Bednarik roared out of the University of Pennsylvania in 1949 as a much ballyhooed, two-time All American. Chuck took the uniform No. 60 and never relinquished it, though he did manage to switch stadiums while a Bird. The '49 Eagles played their home games cross-town in North Philly at Connie Mack Stadium. However, in 1957, Chuck returned to his old stomping grounds when the Eagles switched their home field to Franklin Field. His alma mater's gridiron served as the Eagles' home field till 1970.

"Legend" is an overused term in sport circles. In most cases, it is effusive and unmerited. "Legend," however, fits Chuck Bednarik like a glove. If Chuck Bednarik's career and accomplishments served as the standard for bestowing the term, only a handful of others who ever played the game could qualify.

HOW WELL DO YOU KNOW YOUR BIRDS?

Who was the first Eagles linebacker other than Chuck Bednarik to be selected to the Pro Bowl?

a) Maxie Baughan   b) Chuck Weber
c) Bill Bergey   d) Bob Pellegrini
e) Bill Koman   f) Dave Lloyd
g) Wayne Robinson   h) Tim Rossovich
i) Steve Zabel   j) John Bunting
k) Frank LeMaster

MEET CHUCK BEDNARIK

Charles Philip Bednarik was born in Bethlehem, Pennsylvania, on May 1, 1925—a fitting birth date for a guy who made a career of wreaking May-day-caliber havoc on the gridiron. Chuck grew up tough in the steel town of Bethlehem. He starred in baseball, football, and basketball in high school. In his senior year, Chuck's high school basketball team lost the state finals in the game's final seconds. After high school, Chuck headed off to World War II and flew 30 aerial combat missions. As a member of the Army Air Corps, Chuck's battle record earned him the Air Medal. He returned stateside after being discharged and sought counsel from his high school football coach, who introduced

After Chuck Bednarik (No. 60) knocks the New York Giants' Frank Gifford unconscious late in the fourth quarter, Chuck Weber dives on the ball and the Eagles gain possession. *AP Images*

him to George Munger, Penn's football coach. Chuck went to Penn and became a huge star in the days when the Quakers routinely outdrew the Eagles by embarrassing orders of magnitude. "We used to attract crowds of 70,000 out to Franklin Field," Chuck asserts. "Then I came to the Eagles and 20,000 people would trickle into the stands. Hell, we played the championship game in L.A. my rookie year. There were only 22,000 people in the stands. We played in a driving rainstorm, but could you imagine only 22,000 people showing up for a Super Bowl nowadays?"

The Eagles drafted Chuck first in his senior year via the so-called bonus selection. Every franchise drew a piece of paper from a pile. The one that drew the piece that wasn't blank got to pick before the official draft began. As fate would have it, the defending champion Philadelphia Eagles won the draw. So much for the parity aspirations of the draft— hence the bonus selection was scrabbed as a failed measure. The Birds picked Chuck Bednarik instead of the more nationally recognized Doak Walker of Texas. Both men wound up in the NFL Hall of Fame, yet no one would dispute that Bednarik was not the superior choice.

By itself, a pro football career in Bednarik's era didn't put enough food on the table—and certainly not enough for someone with Chuck's appetite. Indeed, it wasn't until 1961, once 35-year-old Chuck Bednarik had become the biggest name in all of football, that his annual salary topped $20,000. Chuck became the first NFL lineman to break that barrier. Practically every pro footballer held an off-season job. Chuck's job was with Warner Concrete—hence the name "Concrete Charley."

Chuck's greatest renown and most enduring legacy revolves around the number 60. Not only did he wear that number on his jersey, but he also earned the tag of pro football's last "60 Minute Man." Legends are funny things. Some lose all relevance and veracity. Others manage to retain their essence despite the distortions of time and constant retelling. Such is the case with Chuck's "60 Minute Man" tag. Chuck never actually played a full 60 minutes in any contest in 1960. He did toil for 50-plus minutes in several key stretch games during the Birds' 1960 championship run. And, of course, No. 60 saw virtual nonstop action in the '60 championship match itself against the Packers.

Chuck played football bigger than big. He missed but three games in his entire pro career. He missed only one collegiate contest. In the NFL, he played in eight pro bowls, copping the MVP in the '54 game. Nine times he was honored with All-NFL selections. In 1960, his most storied campaign, Chuck started the season at offensive guard, but was moved to linebacker when Bob Pellegrini was injured. Eagles coach Buck Shaw tapped Bednarik as Pellegrini's replacement, even though a few weeks earlier the mentor had dismissed Bednarik as "too old for linebacking." Pundits had been clamoring all season to install No. 60 to bolster the Birds' wobbly, porous defense. In the Giants game, New York middle linebacker Sam Huff and the fabled Giant D was pulverizing QB Norm Van Brocklin with punishing blitzes the entire first half. In the second half, Shaw inserted Bednarik at center and the offense rallied to win.

Chuck had been wooed out of retirement after the 1959 season in what hindsight reveals as the seminal move leading to the 1960 championship. He was again wooed out of retirement after the 1960 championship became a reality. By 1962, he had survived enough NFL bedlam. Chuck called it quits for good. In the ensuing years, he devoted himself to a number of different endeavors. He worked with the concrete company as well as did some sports announcing on TV. He also coached.

These days, Chuck is retired. He and his wife, Emma, live near Bethlehem, Pennsylvania. Chuck can usually be found at Lehigh University's Goodman Stadium on fall Saturdays, cheering on the Lehigh Brown and White.

BUILDING UP TO THE GAME

After losing the '60 opener to the Cleveland Browns, the Eagles went on a tear. They rolled to six straight victories, which propelled them into first place. Their two main challengers, the Browns and the New York Giants, were heavy favorites to win the Eastern Conference. At 5-1-1, the Giants were right on the Eagles' tails. The Browns, with two losses, were not far behind.

The heavy underdog Birds were heading up the Turnpike to take on the big bad Giants in Yankee Stadium. The Giants had dominated the then-47-year-long rivalry. Going into this pivotal 1960 contest, the Giants led the series 33-18-1. The Birds hadn't beaten the Giants in New York since 1952.

The New York press was forecasting a Giants victory. The Giants had thus far been lethargic in the 1960 campaign. However, NY's victory over the Steelers in the final minute the previous week was hyped as the spark that would ignite the squad's run to a championship. In the Steelers' win, Pat Summerall kicked a 37-yard field goal with 30 seconds left to seal the victory. Frank Gifford gathered in two TD passes from QB Charley Conerly and the NY offense seemed to hit on all cylinders for the first time all season. The bad news for New Yorkers was that Conerly was injured and listed as a doubtful starter for the upcoming Eagles contest.

THE GAME OF MY LIFE
NOVEMBER 20, 1960

Chuck Bednarik: "That stadium was packed! [Attendance was 63,571.] It was always tough to play in New York, and I think all the guys who played in New York always had a big advantage. Those guys got the big, national names and recognition and endorsements. I resented that, and it always gave me incentive to play harder when we were up there. Anyway, we didn't start too good that day. You'll have to excuse me. It's tough to remember all the details. Hey, you come back when you're 81 and we'll see how good your memory is, Bob! Anyway, the Giants scored in the first quarter. We were down 7-0, and then in the second quarter, their punter, Don Chandler—you had to watch that guy, he always had something up his sleeve—faked a punt. That kind of embarrassed us because he took the ball all the way down the field [to the Eagles' 15]. But we stopped them without a touchdown. [Summerall kicked a 26-yard field goal.]

"Then we got the ball back on offense and did nothing. They were blitzing Van Brocklin and really giving him a tough time. [Van Brocklin ended the first half a pitiful 1-6 passing. He lost 31 yards on sacks.] Our offense couldn't get going at all. We had to punt the ball back to them. They got the ball and went all the way down the field as the half was winding down. [The Giants took the ball from their own 38-yard line to the Eagles' 6-inch line.] Then the Giants made a mistake. They went for six points instead of taking three for a field goal. They handed the ball to Gifford and we stopped him. [Gene Johnson, a defensive back, came up and made a great stop on Gifford.]

"We went into that locker room after the first half realizing we were getting beat bad, but we were only down 10-0, so we were still very much in the game. [The Giants had 208 first-half yards to the Eagles' 31.] And we decided during the halftime that I would go in and replace Bill Lapham at center. I had started at linebacker, but Buck [Shaw, the Eagles coach] asked me to go both ways like I did against Cleveland the week before. So I did. Our biggest job was to stop the Giants' blitz. That's what I was put at center for.

"The first play when I went out on to the field at center, I told Sam Huff, the Giants' middle linebacker, 'Well, Sam, the fun's over—the veterans are taking over now.' People think I had it out for Sam Huff. I didn't. I like Sam, but I was mad 'cause they had run this show on TV, *The Violent World of Sam Huff*, and Sam became this big name. He got all that exposure 'cause he was playing in New York.

"We didn't exactly jump right out and turn the game around right away. We didn't do anything on our first possession. The Giants got the ball and moved down the field, but then Summerall missed one [a 26-yard FG]. Then we got the offense going. I'll tell you one thing, it was tough to stop Van Brocklin for a whole game. He'd figure you out eventually. You couldn't stop him for a full game. We drove the length of the field. Dutch ran all quick-release plays and draws. He was calling audible after audible. The guy could really read defenses. It got to be a guessing game between Van Brocklin and Huff, and Huff lost. We scored when Van Brocklin threw a [25-yard] TD to Tommy McDonald.

"I think Summerall missed another field goal after that. [Summerall missed a 39-yarder.] That's one of the things that people forget about that game. Their kicker missed a lot of field goals. If he had made them, we'd have lost. But then again, we had a field goal blocked, too. [The Giants blocked a Bobby Walston field goal attempt.] So after Summerall missed another field goal attempt, we finally came down the field and tied when Bobby Walston hit a short field goal.

"When the Giants had the ball, I had a real good shot at Mel Triplett, one of their running backs. He went into the line, I hit him, and the ball popped up. One of our guys [defensive back Jimmy Carr] grabbed the ball and ran it in for a [38-yard] touchdown.

"The next time the Giants got the ball, the game was winding down. They were seven points behind and driving. Their quarterback [George Shaw, who was replacing the injured Charley Conerly] spotted Gifford over the middle and got him the ball. Frank was breaking toward the sideline, trying to juke Don Burroughs, our safety. He didn't see me and I just leveled him. Frank fumbled and Chuck Weber recovered it, and the game was over. You know, in that famous photo of me standing over Frank with my fist raised, that's what I was doing. I didn't know Frank was unconscious. I was just happy 'cause the game was over and we won. I was yelling, 'This @#$! game is over!'

"Anyway, we ran the clock out and won that game. It was a thrill for me. I just knew we were going all the way after that game. And poor Frank, well, you know Frank has never denied that it was a fair hit. It was a good, solid one, not a dirty one. For years afterwards, Frank and I would appear at banquets together and we'd talk about that hit. One time when I was speaking and Frank was on the program, I had them do something special. When they announced me as the speaker, I had them turn all the lights out as I walked to the podium. When I got there, they brought the lights back on and I said, 'Remember that feeling, Frank?'"

WRAP

The Eagles went on to beat the Giants 31-23 the following week when the Giants visited Franklin Field. The Birds wasted little time clinching the conference crown the very next week, beating the St. Louis Cardinals 20-6.

"HOW WELL DO YOU KNOW YOUR BIRDS?" ANSWER
g) Wayne Robinson (in the year 1954)

Chapter 6

BILL CAMPBELL

"SO, WHAT WAS THE GAME OF YOUR LIFE?"

Bill Campbell: "I saw so many great games, so many great performances, over all those years. But the game that sticks out—and actually, I mean this game sticks out by far, nothing even close—is the 1960 NFL championship game. There are several reasons why. First of all, I had been the broadcaster for so many bad teams and so many losing games! And I mean losing teams in every sport—baseball, football, and basketball. So this team was a breath of fresh air. And then, too, there was the personality of the team itself. You had to love them. Without question, I was closer to the 1960 Eagles than any team ever before or since. I made a lot of close friends, but none as close as quarterback Norm Van Brocklin. Anyway, the whole crew was personable and friendly, and at a personal level, I just wanted them to succeed. When they went all the way to the top, I was as thrilled as any guy on the team."

Bill Campbell's voice is instantly identifiable to Philadelphia sport fans from practically every era. His play calling is the verbal thread that weaves through some of the town's most enduring moments. Campbell, who broadcast for the Eagles from 1952 to 1966, was the man behind the mike at their 1960 NFL championship victory. He did the play-by-play for Jim Bunning's perfect game on Father's Day in 1964. He called the play-by-play for Wilt Chamberlain's 100-points-in-a-single-game feat in Hershey—an effort that

41

remains the standard for point production, despite a 2005 challenge by another Philadelphian, Kobe Bryant (though Kobe chooses to dismiss his Philadelphia connection). As a Laker, Bryant poured in 81 points against the Toronto Raptors for basketball's second-highest, single-game, individual production number.

Bill Campbell's heyday behind the mike occurred when football was a small-potatoes proposition compared to the mega-media-circus status it enjoys today. That arrangement allowed Bill to nurture a more intimate relationship with the team and the fans. Present-day boothsters are further removed. They're also paid more, a fact that assuages the grief of losing that connection. In Bill's glory days, his voice channeled all the action to hometown fans when home games were blacked out—a hardship that's difficult to envision for this generation of camera phone text messagers. The play-by-play description alone fired the fans' imaginations and provided the kindling that lit the raging wildfire of fan interest that burns today.

HOW WELL DO YOU KNOW YOUR BIRDS?

Which one of these Eagles running backs became a broadcaster for the Eagles after playing for the 1960 championship team (but not *in* the 1960 championship game)?

a) Theron Sapp   b) Billy Ray Barnes
c) Ted Dean   d) Clarence Peaks

MEET BILL CAMPBELL

"I was born in Philadelphia. I'm a Philadelphian through and through," Bill Campbell chuckles.

Granted, many prominent, expatriate Philadelphians contend that Philly is a state of mind that is not bound by its geography. Today, Bill Campbell resides in New Jersey. But his heart forever belongs to Philly— as do the hearts of Bill Cosby, Kevin Bacon, Will Smith, and a host of other emigrants whose cupboards are still stocked with Tastykakes. "I grew up in Philly and went to several schools around the area, like Archmere Academy in Delaware and Roman Catholic. You can read all about my early life in my new book, *Bill Campbell: the Voice of*

Philadelphia Sports." Bill is an unabashed promoter of author Sam
Carchidi's opus, which tells Campbell's life story.

By virtue of being there, Bill Campbell is the dean of Philly sport
voices. He is perhaps the last Philly play-by-play man who will ever be the
voice of a few professional Philly franchises simultaneously. The march of
specialization blankets the world of sports. The Phillies' current and
longtime play-by-play broadcasting team is locked into baseball, as are
the Eagles' and Sixers' broadcasters. It's unlikely that Harry Kalas or Chris
Wheeler or Merrill Reese will ever do play-by-play for the Phils and the
Eagles and the Sixers. But Bill Campbell did. In fact, he did the Phillies
and Eagles in the same season. He was the main messenger for the pain
and the glory of Phillysport for over half a century. Sixty-six years—that's
the current length of his Philly broadcasting resume.

"I was there for virtually everything," he muses. "When you say
glory and pain, unfortunately the pain outweighed the glory by far! I was
the Phils' play-by-play guy during the '64 collapse. That was painful, but
no more than the 9-73 NBA season I broadcast for the Sixers in '72-'73."

Bill Campbell has always been a broadcaster. He kicked off his career
at the age of 17. "My first job was as a broadcaster," he recalls. "I was in
high school at the time, and honest, the job I got had to be the greatest
job in the world! I worked for WFPG at Steele Pier in Atlantic City in
1940. They paid me $15 a week. A guy named George Thomas hired me.
I think George made $20 a week. We broadcast all the big bands of the
day. These people were the superstars of their time. It was fabulous, a
dream job for a teenager. Glenn Miller, Harry James, the Dorseys—I saw
them all. And the bands were fronted by singers like Frank Sinatra and
Perry Como. I did that job for two summers. Then I graduated high
school and took a position broadcasting for the Lancaster Red Roses, a
Class B minor-league team in Lancaster, Pennsylvania. Billy Rogell and
George Kell, an eventual Hall of Famer, were both there at the time with
Lancaster. Frank Reagan, the football star from Penn, was our catcher.
That's how I got my start broadcasting sports, and I never left the booth."

Bill Campbell's work in broadcasting has been widely recognized.
Among his many honors, he has been the recipient of the Gowdy Media
Award and has been inducted into Basketball Hall of Fame. He was
named Broadcaster of the Year by the National Sports Broadcasters
Association. In 1989, he received the Philadelphia Sportswriters Award

for Outstanding Service. In addition, he belongs to the Philadelphia and Pennsylvania Sports Halls of Fame.

BUILDING UP TO THE GAME

"The championship game was played on Monday, the day after Christmas. Christmas came on Sunday in 1960," Bill Campbell recalls. "Following Christmas just added an extra touch of drama and excitement. The week before the game, Philly had been shut down by a huge snowstorm. … In fact, the team couldn't even practice outside all week. The snow forced them inside. They wound up holding practices in the Palestra. What that meant was that the guys ended up playing a lot more basketball than football all week. But then again, coach Buck Shaw wasn't a big stickler for practice—although in reality, that team was more Van Brocklin's team than Buck's.

"As I said, I was close to Dutch [as Norm Van Brocklin was called]. We used to do a weekly radio show together. I learned more about the game of football from Dutch on that show than I learned in 52 years of covering the game. We looked at film from the week before and analyzed it. Naturally, the games we analyzed all had my play-by-play commentary. He corrected me on everything I had said! Fortunately, the show was pre-taped, because Dutch would really let me have it. He had a kind of grizzly personality. For the first few weeks, I thought he was the most miserable guy in the world. But as time went by, I saw that not only did he know the game better than any football player I ever met, but he also was a nice guy. He was tough, but he let you know exactly where he stood on everything. And he was so determined to win in '60. He was determined '60 would be his final season and he would go out on top. So when I look back on that 1960 championship game, I think of it as a tribute to a guy who simply refused to lose. If it's possible to win by sheer strength of will, Dutch did."

Strong will notwithstanding, it was the efficacy of Dutch's will that was in question in the 1960 season opener. The contest was ugly. Cleveland humiliated the Birds 41-24 in front of 56,303 fans who entered Franklin Field that day as believers. The Eagles' surprising 1959 campaign had generated high hopes. They had climbed out of the basement into a second-place tie with the mighty Browns. However, after the shellacking in the opener, most fans walked out of Franklin Field as doubters.

Pro football itself had taken a quantum leap in popularity two years earlier. That's when the Johnny Unitas-led Baltimore Colts engineered a sudden-death victory over the New York Giants. The battle captivated primetime American TV viewers and plunged professional football deeper into the national consciousness than ever before. The game of football—or, more accurately, the business/enterprise/industry of football—was changing radically. Coaches like Paul Brown and Vince Lombardi converted football from a seasonal distraction into a full-year, full-throttle entertainment juggernaut. The combatants had a different look, too. Jimmy Brown was the poster guy for the new game. Brown redefined the running back position. Immensely powerful at 232 pounds and enormously oversized compared to his peers and predecessors, Brown was the prototype of the modern running back. He packaged speed, power, and agility. Those skills were considered mutually exclusive prior to Brown's assault on the NFL record book. Strange thinking, I know, but smoking was considered cool in those days, too.

Returning to the 1960 opener, the Eagles and their fans had the painful opportunity to witness every one of Jimmy Brown's marvelous attributes in its full glory. He and fellow future Hall of Fame running back Bobby Mitchell (who would gain fame a few years later by catching Sonny Jurgensen aerials in Washington) ran wild. Mitchell gained 156 yards on 14 carries; Brown racked up 153 yards on 24 totes. After their abysmal debut, the Birds rattled off nine consecutive victories to run away with the conference title. Their feat astounded the sport world, but few football experts believed they were for real.

Philly's Western Conference opponent turned out to be the Green Bay Packers. The Packers had also resurrected and reinvented themselves. They too had finished last two years before on a pathetic 1-10-1 log. The following year, the Pack was back, improving to 7-5—a mark identical with the '59 Eagles.' Green Bay's coach and change agent was Vince Lombardi. Lombardi, the former Fordham Block of Granite, coached his 1960 charges to their first conference title since the franchise's glory years in the late '30s and mid-'40s.

The '60 Packers had power and depth. They also had glitz. Paul Hornung, their halfback, was the golden boy from Notre Dame. He was a bachelor and one of the game's carousing bad boys. He was also a media darling. How much of a darling? A few years earlier at Notre Dame, Hornung became the only member of a losing team ever to win the Heisman Trophy.

The Pack swaggered into Phillytown for the championship game as a heavy favorite. Even in hindsight—actually, particularly in hindsight— that's not surprising. Thirteen of the aggressive, young, Lombardi-dynasty Packers would wind up in the Hall of Fame. In contrast, the Eagles were fronted by a 35-year-old, Chuck Bednarik, and 34-year-old Norm Van Brocklin. Bednarik was forced to pull double duty, playing both offense and defense, because frankly, the Eagles ranks were so thin. Norm Van Brocklin had his sights set on retirement after the game.

After the bitter cold and snow of a harsh pre-championship week, Monday, December 26, 1960, dawned mild and sunny—as ideal a theatre for football as Phillydom can provide in its deep and dark Decembers. The temperature was 40 degrees at high noon with a light 10-to 15-mile-per-hour wind. By the way, high noon is not a dramatic device in this instance. That was the actual game start time. Franklin Field, packed to the rafters with 67,325 spectators (contrasted with the 6,732,500 who would lay subsequent claim to having been present), had been cleared of snow the week before. Both teams took the field at full strength. No key players were injured or missing in action.

THE GAME OF MY LIFE
DECEMBER 26, 1960

Bill Campbell: "There were so many big plays. Things started off badly for us that day. We got the ball first on a Hornung kickoff, and three plays later the Packers had it back. Dutch had tossed a little flare pass that went right to their big end [Bill Quinlan]. I think it surprised Quinlan. [Quinlan was even more surprised when he ended up in Eagle green a season later, but not nearly as surprised as Eagles fans were at the drop-off in his performance.] But then, all of a sudden, whaddya know, the Packers are inside the 15-yard line and the game hasn't even really started.

"Lombardi, I think, sensed blood at that point. He tried a fourth-and-1 play from scrimmage instead of getting on the board with a field goal. The Packers were known for their toughness and line play. Not only that, they had one of the most bruising runners in the world, Jim Taylor, at fullback. They handed the ball to Jim, who plowed up into the middle and the Eagles stopped him. That was the story of the game right there. Those Eagles were the original bend-but-not-break defense. That stop was a huge play and a big boost for the home team.

"After they stopped Taylor, I remember the Eagles offense couldn't get started. But I knew it was a matter of time with Dutch. It really was. I know I'm repeating myself, but if ever a football player won a championship game on pure will, Dutch did. He just refused to lose that game. He refused to let his final opportunity slip away. He and Chuck Bednarik were hardened vets. They both knew how tough it was—what a long road it was—to make it to the championship game. They were both near the end of their careers. Both planned to retire after the game. Chuck was wooed back, but Dutch stuck to his retirement plans. Of course, he was replaced by another Hall of Fame QB, Sonny Jurgensen, but the Eagles lost a lot when they lost Dutch's leadership. ...

"The strength of will that those two guys, Bednarik and Van Brocklin, imparted to their teammates was an intangible. It simply can't be undervalued as a factor in that game.

"Another big moment I remember so well was when 'Squeaky' caught a TD pass—a 35-yarder. Squeaky was a nickname Dutch gave to Tommy McDonald. That TD pass just proved something that Dutch always told me. He used to say, 'If Squeaky comes into the huddle and tells me he's got his man beat, the game becomes easy: all I have to do is keep tossing him the ball.' Well, that's what happened. McDonald got free for a 22-yarder, scampered back to the huddle, and said he had his guy beat. Dutch came right back with the long TD. What a pretty sight—Tommy in the corner of that end zone, slipping into the snow the ground crew had pushed over to the side of the field. When Tommy tumbled after scoring, it looked like all of Philadelphia was there to help him up. The fans and police were lifting Tommy up and congratulating him. What a moment for the city!

"I remember our final scoring drive and our final score. That's another indelible memory: Ted Dean, our young local back from Radnor, carried one in. It was the winning score. Ted drove right over a lineman named Gerry Huth on a sweep that looked like it was drawn up in the Packers' playbook.

"Of course, the Packers weren't about to lie down. They fought and fought. There was no quit in a Lombardi team. At the end of the game, the Packers were driving and it looked like they were going to score. Actually, it was a coming-of-age kind of day for Bart Starr. He was young at the time, but on that final drive you could see he had what it takes to be something special. Anyway, with just a few seconds left, Starr tossed the ball out to Taylor, who careened off a few guys and then got wrapped up by Bednarik. Chuck just sat on him as the clock ticked off, with Taylor squirming and kicking and cussing. Chuck never let him up, and that was it. Eagles win. The fans swarmed the field. The goalposts came down. Philly went crazy. And, wow, it's hard to believe it was all so long ago and that it hasn't happened again since."

"HOW WELL DO YOU KNOW YOUR BIRDS?" ANSWER
d) Clarence Peaks

Chapter 7

JIM SKAGGS

"SO, WHAT WAS THE GAME OF YOUR LIFE?"

Jim Skaggs: "My days with the Eagles seem like such a long, long time ago, especially when I'm out shoveling snow here in the state of Washington. I had wonderful days in Philly, mostly because of the fine group of guys I played with. As for the game of my life, let me see. ... You know, I'd have to say that the game of my life came relatively early in my career against the Detroit Lions. It wasn't a big game or an important game. To be honest, we didn't get a chance to play too many big or significant games in those days. The Eagles teams I played for didn't have very good won-lost records. But I kind of feel that I arrived as a pro, for want of a better term, in the game against Detroit. So yeah, I'd pick that game as the game of my life."

Jim Skaggs toiled in Philadelphia's offensive trenches for 10 seasons, protecting a multitude of quarterbacks like Norm Snead, King Hill, Jack Concannon, George Mira, Rick Arrington, Pete Liske, and John Reaves. Skaggs was a much sought-after lineman following his days at the University of Washington. After college, he made the coast-to-coast trip to the Quaker City to play with the Eagles and never left town. Jim was shuffled in and out of the starting lineup at both guard and tackle throughout his career. He played with the Birds in some lean years; however, Jim Skaggs kept a positive attitude—a trait he carries still.

HOW WELL DO YOU KNOW YOUR BIRDS?

The Eagles boast one amazing three-year stretch where the NFL leader in pass receptions each season was a Philadelphia Eagle. Even more amazingly, it was a different Eagle each of the three years. Who were the three Eagles receivers? (Pick three from the list below.)

Part A

a) Bobby Walston
b) Harold Carmichael
c) Don Zimmerman
d) Pete Retzlaff
e) Harold Jackson
f) Charle Young
g) Pete Pihos
h) Tommy McDonald
i) Ben Hawkins
j) Jack Ferrante
k) Charley Gauer
l) Ron Goodwin
m) Mike Ditka
n) Charlie Smith
o) Keith Krepfle
p) John Spagnola
q) Mike Quick
r) Fred Barnett

OK (or not ...), now what were the three consecutive years that these three different Eagles led the league in receptions?

Part B

a) 1947, 1948, 1949
b) 1948, 1949, 1950
c) 1957, 1958, 1959
d) 1958, 1959, 1960
e) 1959, 1960, 1961
f) 1972, 1973, 1974
g) 1978, 1979, 1980
h) 1989, 1989, 1990
i) 1994, 1995, 1996
j) 2000, 2001, 2002

MEET JIM SKAGGS

When James Lee Skaggs, born January 3, 1940, in Wetumka, Oklahoma, graduated from the University of Washington in 1962, he had a choice to make. "I guess you could say they were unusual days in the history of football," Jim reflects. "The American Football League had started up in 1960. That started an all-out bidding war between the two pro leagues. The good thing about all that was that the bidding started to drive football salaries up. When I graduated, the Eagles drafted me in the NFL and the Oakland Raiders drafted me in the AFL. I had to decide where to go. To tell the truth, the AFL wasn't well established in 1962. For some reason, it didn't seem like the AFL was in the same league with the NFL, so I went with the Eagles. I have no regrets. I enjoyed my time in Philadelphia."

Things got busy right away for the ex-Husky. After the regular collegiate season, he played in the East-West Shrine Game, the Hula Bowl, and the Coaches All-America Bowl. Unfortunately, as it turned out, another of his postseason commitments was the College All-Star Game.

"Playing in the College All-Star Game included a 10-day training camp," Jim recalls. "I broke my ankle in the camp. I didn't play in the game, which would have been a thrill and an honor. The Green Bay Packers were the NFL champs that year. They were our opponents. I would love to have played against that great team with Paul Hornung, Bart Starr, Jim Taylor, and all those other great names. As it was, I missed the College All-Star game and then reported to the Eagles' training camp in Hershey, Pennsylvania, in a full leg cast. I sat out my whole first season on injured reserve."

Jim's problems didn't end when his ankle healed. When 1963 rolled around, the 6-foot-3, 250-pound athlete had earned a starting slot at tackle when he ripped his left knee apart and missed the rest of the season.

Skaggs didn't miss much. The '63 Birds fluttered to a 2-10 record under head coach Nick Skorich. When 1964 rolled around, the Birds had a new look. Coach Joe Kuharich had taken over, and Jim Skaggs was set to begin his pro career in earnest.

"We finished 6-8 in '64. That doesn't sound impressive, but our team showed what I felt was promise," Jim analyzes. "Sure, we lost eight games, but seven of those losses were by a touchdown or less. To my thinking, that '64 season was really my rookie season. I had only played a few games the year before. In '64, I started at offensive guard. We had some good players on the roster that year. We had drafted Bob Brown, who became an all-time great, and we had a good backfield with Ollie Matson, Timmy Brown, and Earl Gros. And when Norm Snead had time, he could throw the football as well as anyone."

The 1965 Eagles slipped back to 5-9, but reversed that log to 9-5 in 1966. Unfortunately, that was the sole winning season Jim Skaggs enjoyed as a pro. By 1968, No. 70 had lost his starting job to Mark Nordquist. He regained the starting slot in 1969 under new head coach

Jerry Williams. Jim was again a starter in 1970, but became more of a spot starter in his final two campaigns in 1970 and 1971.

After his pro career ended, Jim set out on a 29-year second career with State Farm Insurance. These days, Jim is living on his little 33-acre farm in God's country, not far from Spokane, Washington. He's enjoying life—even when life forces him to step outside the warmth of his homestead to clear snow off the roadway with his tractor. That's what he was doing one Sunday last winter when I spoke with him. "Still spending your weekend afternoons pushing heavy stuff around, eh Jim?" I asked. Jim Skaggs didn't drop a beat. "Old habits die hard," he chuckled.

BUILDING UP TO THE GAME

The promise of 1964 blossomed into an opening-day victory at Franklin Field in front of 54,260 Iggles fans. Unfortunately, the season deteriorated quickly in the wake of the 1-0 start. The Birds lost six of the next seven and effectively fell out of contention. Cleveland was the class of the Eastern Conference. The Browns left everyone in their dust as they blasted to an 11-3 campaign.

The Eagles finally achieved their second victory, a 21-14 yawner against the Washington Redskins, in the ninth contest of the campaign. From there on out to the finish, the Eagles alternated wins. When the season finale rolled around against the Detroit Lions, the Eagles, who had nothing to gain, were still hungry for wins. So were their fans. On December 19, 1965, Franklin Field welcomed 56,718 Philly faithful to see a "meaningless" contest between the 5-7-1 Lions from Motown and the 5-8 Eagles from the Quaker City. (To show how committed Philly fans are compared to those of other cities, in the Birds' previous two away-game tilts, both meaningless contests, 28,706 fans showed up in St. Louis and 22,002 showed up in Pittsburgh.) As Jim Skaggs told me, "There was no such thing as a meaningless game to me." Evidently not. The "meaningless" game against the Lions that day is the game of Jim Skaggs' life.

THE GAME OF MY LIFE
DECEMBER 19, 1965

Jim Skaggs: "We had a disappointing season in '65, no question about it. The Browns were hot. Jimmy Brown was at the peak of his career. Cleveland started hot, and once we started to slide, we never really got untracked till it was too late. Still, we knew we had talent and we knew we were a lot better than our record indicated. And we were confident that we would turn things around the next year.

"I was in my second 'real' season in '65. I missed my first two NFL seasons because of injury. In '64, I was a rookie for all practical purposes. I started and played every game—same as I did in '65. But not too many people knew me outside Philadelphia, so I was excited about the Lions game. You know why? Because I was going up against Alex Karras. Do you remember Alex Karras? He was as good a lineman as there was. [Yes, he was. Famed for his role as Mongo in Mel Brooks' classic *Blazing Saddles*, Karras, interestingly enough, also sat out the 1963 season. Commissioner Pete Rozelle suspended Alex and Packer Paul Hornung for betting on NFL games. Both were reinstated after a year's suspension.] Anyway, I was determined to have a good game against this guy because he was considered the best."

"It wasn't our day, unfortunately. Detroit got out early and never looked back. They had that old Cleveland quarterback, Milt Plum [also a former Penn State QB and Woodbury High grad]. Plum threw an early TD pass to Jim Gibbons, a guy who played for Detroit for years. Then Detroit scored again [on a 1-yard run by Tom Nowatzke] and we were down 14-0.

"I think we might have come back a little then [correct: the Eagles scored a TD on a 9-yard pass from Norm Snead to Ollie Matson], but Detroit matched us. That's kind of the way the game went. The Lions answered every time we threatened. But the thing that makes the game memorable to me was that I had a good game against Alex Karras. But that doesn't mean I had an entire good game. I had a rough start! The first play of the game, I never saw anybody move so fast! Karras was by me before I even got out of my stance. I mean that literally.

"This happened to be the first game I ever remember where they used film—or maybe it was tape—of the action as it happened. We went in at halftime, and Nick Skorich and our coaches grabbed me and showed me the film. They said, 'You've gotta get out of your stance faster!' That's easier said than done, but somehow I managed to do it. I concentrated on getting out of my stance and moving in on Alex. Well, my performance was nothing miraculous, but it was satisfying. I slowed him down. We lost the game, but I felt I had contributed and I certainly had given everything I had in the process. I think that spirit carried through with the whole squad next year. And it was very gratifying … because Alex complimented my play after the game. Coming from him, that was quite a tribute."

WRAP

After Matson scored for the Eagles, Detroit answered with a 31-yard TD pass from Plum to John Henderson. Prior to the end of the half, the Eagles returned fire with a 2-yard TD run by Tim Brown.

In the second half, the Lions extended their 21-14 lead by seven when cornerback Dick LeBeau ran an interception back 30 yards for a TD. However, the Birds fought back with two consecutive scores—the first on a 63-yard punt return by Bob Shann, the second on a 9-yard Snead to Ron Goodwin connection.

Running back Tom Nowatzke took a 22-yard Plum pass to pay dirt and seal the contest, ending the year on a down note.

"HOW WELL DO YOU KNOW YOUR BIRDS?" ANSWER
Part A: e) Harold Jackson, **b)** Harold Carmichael,
f) Charle Young.
Part B: f) 1972, 1973, 1974

Chapter 8

TIM BROWN

"SO, WHAT WAS THE GAME OF YOUR LIFE?"

Tim Brown: "That's a tough one, Bob. I had a lot of big games. I think I ran five kickoffs and one punt back for TDs. Every time you do something like that, it's a big game—one you never forget. But when I have to pick the game of my life, I'm torn between two. The first game was the opener in 1961. I ran a 105-yard kickoff back in that one. I hadn't played much till then. I was mostly on the bench. I was on the 1960 championship team, but I didn't get much playing time. When I ran that kickoff back, it kick-started the Eagles' 1961 season, but it also kick-started my career. … After that game, the coaches started to try to utilize me more. I started getting much more playing time. Still, taking everything into consideration, I think the game against Dallas when I ran two kickoffs back for touchdowns has to be the game of my life. Besides, there's some interesting background I can talk about for that one, too."

Tim Brown was one of the most exciting running backs ever to juke his way into the hearts of the Quaker City faithful. Tim's gridiron accomplishments and records rebut assertions suggesting that Vince Lombardi was infallible in matters relating to football. Lombardi released Tim Brown from the Packers. In doing so, Green Bay's legendary coach provided the Philadelphia Eagles with the lion's share of their offense for the first half of the '60s.

HOW WELL DO YOU KNOW YOUR BIRDS?

Only two Eagles running backs have been selected to the Pro Bowl three times. Tim Brown is one. Who is the other?

a) Wilbert Montgomery   b) Billy Barnes
c) Steve Van Buren   d) Brian Westbrook
e) Clarence Peaks   f) Tom Sullivan
g) Ricky Watters   h) Tom Woodeshick

MEET TIM BROWN

Thomas Allen Brown, born May 24, 1937, was raised in an orphanage (the Soldiers' and Sailors' Children's Home) in Richmond, Indiana. He was given loving guidance by a guardian and, due to that guidance, became one of 17 African Americans in a student body that numbered 3,500 at Ball State Teachers College in Indiana. "I enjoyed my college years," Tim muses. "I wasn't subjected to any racial problems. I was lucky. I was totally accepted. When I was in college, I started a rock group, 'Timmy Brown and the Thunderbirds.' So even though I had to wash dishes and hold down odd jobs to make enough money to get through college, I enjoyed my college years."

After graduation, Tim was a lowly 27th-round draft choice for the Green Bay Packers. "That's when things changed. They had this good ol' boy mentality up there. I wasn't very popular with a lot of the guys who came from the Deep South, and that kind of attitude and treatment was foreign to me. Things were different for African Americans in the NFL in those days. Nobody really talks about the way it was. For one thing, I'm sure there was an unspoken limit of three African Americans per team. Dallas was just starting out in 1960. I remember the first time I saw the Dallas team. They had about nine African Americans on the roster. I had a conversation with [Cleveland great] Jimmy Brown at the time. Jim said, 'You watch. That's gonna change.' Sure enough, next thing I knew, Dallas was down to three African Americans. I always suspected that Pete Rozelle [the NFL commissioner at the time] silently supported that kind of thinking."

Tim Brown wound up in Philadelphia in 1960. He also wound up on the championship roster, although he saw only limited action for the champs. He didn't get a decent opportunity to strut his stuff that year till the Eagles had safely wrapped up the Eastern Conference title. At that point, only two regular-season games remained. Timmy saw significant action in both those games—and he shined. Against Pittsburgh in a driving blizzard, Tim and backup QB Sonny Jurgensen were inserted after the Steelers had built up a 28-0 lead. The Birds battled back to 28-21 when time ran out. Tim played a pivotal role in all three Eagles scores. He scored two of the TDs himself—one on a nifty 52-yard pass-and-run, the other on a 9-yard scoring catch. Although he didn't score the other TD, his 61-yard catch-and-run was the key play of that scoring drive.

The following week, Tim led all Eagles receivers with 128 yards on five receptions. He also gained 25 yards on six carries. In toto, he scored four TDs in those final two games—two by air and two on the ground. Not bad, but apparently not quite enough.

Tim started the following season on the bench again. However, he made himself noticed immediately after the opening gun. In front of 60,671 Franklin Field fans, No. 22 lugged the opening kickoff of the 1961 season back 105 yards for a TD. When the season concluded, he led the entire circuit in number of kickoff returns (29) and yardage on kickoff returns (811). He also started to see more action. From a measly nine carries in 1960, his rushes grew to 50 and his average gain was a glittery 6.8 yards per carry.

Tim Brown burst into full-fledged stardom the following year, 1962. Once more, he flared some opening-day fireworks. This time, he returned a botched field goal attempt 99 yards for six against the stunned St. Louis Cardinals. The following week, Tim caught a pass and scampered 74 yards to pay dirt. Although the Eagles struggled through a horrendous 3-10-1 last-place season, Tim Brown was a shining light. He led the Birds in five categories: 2,306 total yards, 545 rushing yards, 831 yards on kickoff returns, 81 yards on punt returns, and 78 points. His 849 reception yards placed second on the squad behind future Hall of Fame receiver Tommy McDonald.

In 1963, Quaker City fans didn't get their accustomed opening-day Tim Brown show. They had to wait till game two. That's when Tim toted a kickoff back 100 yards against the Cardinals. When Cleveland and Philadelphia squared off a few weeks later, both Browns put on a show. Cleveland's Jimmy Brown broke Joe Perry's NFL record of 8,390 lifetime yards rushing by slashing through the Eagles defense for 144 yards on 25 carries. Meanwhile, the Birds' Tim Brown scrambled the Browns' D for 198 total yards—117 on kickoff returns, 43 on pass receptions, and 38 on rushes from scrimmage.

When the curtain came down on the '63 season, Tim Brown had set the all-time NFL record for total offense, compiling 2,428 yards on runs, catches, and returns. He ended up third in the league in rushing. He and Pete Retzlaff were named to the All-Pro East squad.

Then came 1964, a year that will live in infamy in Philadelphia— and not just for the Phillies. This infamy concerns the Eagles and their new coach, Joe Kuharich. Joe's arrival changed things for Tim Brown. "I had trouble right off the bat," Tim confesses. "The Eagles had helped me get into the National Guard. I had to report to summer camp for two weeks. As a result, I missed the first week of Eagles training camp. When I arrived at camp, they were acting as though I just hadn't reported, like an attitude thing. At our first team meeting, Joe Kuharich announced to the whole team, 'We're not going to have any stars on this team. Do you have any problems with that, Mr. Brown?' I could never let statements like that go by. It's just not my nature. I always had to come back with a comment. So I said, 'I can do that if you just don't give me the ball.' The guys laughed, but Joe Kuharich didn't. Kuharich made up his mind right then and there that he wasn't giving me the ball. I believe I could have had an unbelievable career if they had given me the ball 15 times a game. The problem was, that wasn't the thinking back then. They didn't think I was that kind of back. They thought I lacked durability."

Unfortunately, he was tagged "Little Timmy Brown" early on. He had moves like a scatback. The fact that he had the physique of a big back went unnoticed. At 5-foot-11, Tim was powerfully built and weighed almost 200 pounds. He was larger than most backs of his era. "I think I was cast like 'Little Timmy Brown' as a sort of contrast to my contemporary, Jimmy Brown," Tim suggests. "I was probably bigger than most of the backs I played against, but I looked small compared to Jimmy." Who didn't?

"Little" Timmy Brown earned a berth on the '64 Pro Bowl squad, despite his diminished role in the (alleged) Kuharich system. (He wound up with 52 fewer rushing attempts than the year before.) In '65, Tim "rebounded" and turned in his finest season as a rusher. He finished third in the league in yards gained (861) and led the league in rushing yards per attempt (5.4). His efforts earned him a second-team slot on the All-Pro squad and another trip to the Pro Bowl.

The Eagles all-time record book bears copious testimony to Tim Brown's distinguished career. He ranks 11th on the all-time Eagles' scoring list. Only four other Eagles have scored more TDs than he. He played more games at running back than all but four other Eagles. He ranks sixth on the all-time Eagles' list for yards gained rushing. He shares the sixth slot with Steve Van Buren on the Eagles' all-time list for average gain per rush.

After one season with the Baltimore Colts in 1968, Tim enjoyed a Hollywood film career. He appeared in Robert Altman's *Nashville*. His TV credits include *M*A*S*H*, *Gimme a Break*, and the soap opera *Capitol*. Tim later worked as a correctional officer in Los Angeles, California. Nowadays, he's retired and in excellent health in Palm Springs, California.

BUILDING UP TO THE GAME

"Right after the opener in 1966, I entered the 10,000 yards club," Tim notes. "At that point, there weren't too many other guys who ever played who had gained that many yards. It was a real accomplishment. Remember, we only played 12 games a season."

Despite Tim's 114 yards rushing, the Cardinals squeaked by the Eagles 16-13 to open what looked like another disappointing season. The Birds surprised, however, and turned the season around. They won the next two games over the Falcons and Giants before getting whipped 41-10 in the return engagement with St. Louis. More humiliation awaited the following week, when Dallas destroyed them 56-7. Dallas' 56 points tied for the most points ever scored against the Birds up to that point. (The Giants scored 56 the first time the Philadelphia Eagles ever took the field in 1933.)

The Eagles fought back with wins over the Steelers and Giants before dropping one to the Washington Redskins. Incidentally, Joe Kuharich had traded Sonny Jurgensen to the 'Skins (remember Joe's "no stars" philosophy?), and it was Sonny who engineered the win— Washington's sixth straight win (including exhibition games) since Sonny left Philly.

Dallas was coming to Philadelphia to take on the 4-4 Birds. The game was pivotal for the Eagles if they were to contend. It was also a bit daunting. They had to go up against the 'Boys after the 'Boys had laid a whupping on them in the first tilt.

"The week before the game, one of the Philly reporters interviewed me," Tim Brown reminisces. "He said that Dallas was claiming that I wasn't a threat anymore. I told him that Dallas couldn't stop me if I got the ball in my hands. If the Eagles let me run back kickoffs again, run the ball, and catch the ball, Dallas couldn't stop me everywhere. The day before the game, Joe Kuharich, who, up till then, had been telling the press he was 'preserving me' by not utilizing me more—preserving me for what, I don't know—came up to me and said, 'You're running back kickoffs tomorrow.' Up till then, I hadn't even practiced with the special teams. I think Joe was just hanging me out there."

Joe hung Tim out and Dallas suffered the execution.

THE GAME OF MY LIFE
NOVEMBER 6, 1966

Tim Brown: "Our special teams were great that day. Otherwise, our offense didn't do a thing. Yeah, and our defense too—when they needed to shut Dallas down, they did.

That game didn't start out too promising. Dallas kicked to us. I ran it back—just a normal return, nothing special. But on the first play from scrimmage, we fumbled [Earl Gros was the culprit] and Dallas scored [on the fifth play of the game]. This time when they kicked off, I was ready. I just saw them all rushing down the center of the field, so I started up the middle and then veered over to the sideline. I could run sideways pretty fast. Jimmy Brown complimented me once on my style. He said, 'You run faster sideways than other guys run straight ahead.' I used to practice running sideways when I was in college. I was always making up little games to challenge myself. I used to run down the railroad tracks nearby. I'd try to run sideways and step on every other railroad tie. Then I'd switch the rules and tried to step on every tie. I think that little game helped me running a football. Anyway, that's what happened on that return. I ended up running sideways and breaking out of the pack. I remember beating their last guy, the kicker [Danny Villanueva], and breaking home free. That happened on the next return, too.

"I think Dallas scored again after that. [Actually, Dallas scored twice: once on a Villanueva field goal and once again on a Meredith 1-yard rollout for a TD.] Then they kicked to me again, and I took it back 90 yards. Everything broke fast on that play. I just headed up the middle and veered off slightly and found a hole. Next thing I knew, I was outrunning the kicker again. It sure felt good, considering that Dallas had been saying before the game that they weren't worried about me, that I was kind of washed up.

"We seemed to score all our points in one big bunch at that point. After my score, Dallas had to kick the ball right back to us. One of our rookies [Brown is referring to Aaron Martin, a DB from North Carolina State, who was not actually a rookie: it was his first season of two as a Bird, but he had previously logged one year with the Rams] took the punt and ran it back about 70 yards for a score. [Danny Villanueva also punted for the Cowboys. On the afternoon, Villaneuva suffered the ignominy of watching two of his kickoffs and one of his punts end up in his own end zone.] Sam Baker kicked us a field goal not too long afterwards, and I think that was the end of our scoring for the day. [Yes, it was, Tim.] At that point, our defense rose to the task. They held Dallas the rest of the way. That Dallas offense was tough, too. They had weapons—guys like Robert Hayes, who was considered the 'World's Fastest Human' at that time, and [Don] Meredith, a good QB, and [Dan] Reeves, an underrated runner.

"We did have a big scare at the end of the game, though. Meredith completed a pass to Reeves [who caught it at the 26-yard line with less than a minute to play] and ran it inside the 15. But Joe Scarpati actually stole the ball from him! They could have kicked a field goal and won the game if Joe hadn't forced that turnover, but as it is, we won, and the victory lit our fire the rest of the season. I think we only lost one more game and came close to winning the Eastern Conference. So that was the game of my life. It's always a thrill to run a kickoff back, but to run two of them back in a crucial game against Dallas in front of that wonderful Philly crowd was really over-the-top great."

WRAP

Timmy Brown's skill as a kickoff returner speaks for itself. He ranks No. 1 on the Eagles all-time list in number of kickoff returns (169), kickoff return yards (4,483—almost 1,000 yards ahead of second-place Brian Mitchell), and kickoff return TDs (five). His 287 yards on November 6, 1966, set the Eagles' standard for most kickoff return yards in a single game.

Tim's 287 kickoff return yards also eclipsed the 240 yards that the entire Dallas offense gained that day. If ever there were a contest in which the special teams virtually won a game single-handedly, it was the Eagles-Cowboys tilt on November 6, 1966. The Birds scored all three of their TDs on kickoff returns and a punt return. Otherwise, as the *New York Times* reported, "Looking about as good as a bad high school team when running plays from scrimmage, the Philadelphia Eagles upset the Dallas Cowboys 24-23." The Birds also produced their entire output in the first half—a half when their offense recorded an anemic 6 yards from scrimmage. The Eagles ended the day with only 80 yards of offense, and Tim Brown's 38 rushing yards accounted for essentially half of that. (OK, 47.5 percent for you sticklers.)

In any event, the 60,658 fans that showed up had much to thrill about. They were witnessing NFL history. At that point, Tim was the only guy in NFL history ever to run two kickoffs back in a single game. Those fans also watched the marquee game in the last winning season the Birds would boast for the next 11 years.

Chapter 9

BEN HAWKINS

"SO, WHAT WAS THE GAME OF YOUR LIFE?"

Ben Hawkins: "I had some good games. I think I still rank pretty high on the Eagles all-time list for most single-game receiving yardage in a game against the Cardinals. [Ben's 197 yards against the St. Louis Cardinals on October 22, 1967, is the fifth-best all-time single-game receiving total for the Birds.] One game pops up or really sticks out. That's the game when I caught four touchdowns in one game. That's a day anybody would remember, so that's the game of my life."

Ben Hawkins came to Philadelphia after a stellar career at Arizona State University. Picked in the third round of the '66 draft, his arrival coincided with the zenith of the Joe Kuharich experiment. The Philly club went a surprising 9-5 that year, which tied them with Cleveland for second place in the Eastern Conference. Pete Retzlaff was still the dean of the receiving corps. Pete caught 40 that year, but rookie Ben Hawkins also made his presence felt with 14 receptions. It was the following year, however, when Ben's star rose in the NFL. The 6-foot-1, 180-pound athlete zoomed to No. 1 among all Eagle receivers, nabbing 59 passes for an average of 21.4 yards per catch and a league-leading 1,265 reception yards. Hawkins led the team in receptions the next year as well. In fact, over the next three years, Ben Hawkins never failed to rank among his team's top four receivers.

Ben Hawkins' Philly legacy was that of a tough, physical player with the ability to break a game open any time with a big play. Longtime Philly fans will always remember Ben as the guy with the dangling chin strap that remained unbuckled all game long.

HOW WELL DO YOU KNOW YOUR BIRDS?

Who has the most 100-yard receiving games as an Eagle?

a) Fred Barnet   b) Ben Hawkins
c) Irving Fryar   d) Pete Retzlaff
e) Jack Ferrante   f) Tommy McDonald
g) Pete Pihos   h) Bobby Walston
i) Charles Young   j) Freddie Mitchell
k) Mike Quick

MEET BEN HAWKINS

Benjamin Charles Hawkins was born in Newark, New Jersey, on March 22, 1944. He starred on the gridiron at Nutley High School in New Jersey. After high school, Ben headed west to the desert, where he played ball for Frank Kush at Arizona State University. "Coach Kush wouldn't let us take our helmets off at practice, and it was really hot there in the desert. That's how I got in the habit of not buckling my chin strap," Ben confesses. "That way, I could take my helmet off quick. I could kind of lift it up and put it back down quick. There was lots of padding inside the helmet, so I was pretty safe keeping the chin strap loose. I mean, really, the helmet always stayed pretty solid on my head. Then later on in pro ball, I didn't buckle my chin strap because tacklers sometimes ended up holding my helmet while I was getting away. I scored touchdowns twice in the NFL because of my chin strap being loose. Willie Wood with Green Bay tore my helmet off one time and I got away. Same thing happened with Kermit Alexander of San Francisco. I would take every little advantage I could."

Ben was a *Time Magazine* All-American in his senior year. He earned that recognition by catching 78 balls for 1,222 yards and nine TDs in his final two collegiate campaigns. "I enjoyed my college career," Ben reminisces. "I met lots of great people. Remember Curly Culp? He was a

Wide receiver Ben Hawkins (No. 18) breaks away from linebacker Lee Roy Jordan for a first down in a 1971 game against Dallas. *AP Images*

terrific guy. I roomed with Curly Culp when I was a senior. He was only a sophomore. Curly was also a big NCAA championship wrestler. He became a great lineman for Kansas City in the NFL."

Ben is the first to admit he broke into the NFL not with a bang, but with somewhat of a whimper. He caught 14 passes as a rookie, but that was disappointing output for a receiver of his talent. "I dropped too many passes. I can't explain it," Ben recalls. "I wasn't nervous or anything. I just had trouble holding on to the ball. Why? I don't know." Whatever the cause, he found the antidote his sophomore year, when he turned in what would prove to be his finest pro season ever. Ben set the Eagles mark at the time for most receiving yards ever by an Eagle in a single season. Though the mark has since been eclipsed, No. 18 still ranks in third place on the Eagles' all-time list. He trails only Mike Quick's 1,409 yards in 1983 and Irving Fryar's 1,216 yards in 1997.

Ben never again matched the glitzy figures he threw up as a soph. Unfortunately, his career unfolded during a pretty dismal chapter in Eagles history. He only enjoyed one winning season his entire career—and that one came in his rookie season. Throughout his eight years as a

Bird, Ben played under four different head coaches (Kuharich, Jerry Williams, Ed Khayat, and Mike McCormack). "I think that was one of our major problems. … We had some good players. We just never had stability. We never had the chance to play under the same system very long."

Notwithstanding that barrier, Ben competed at a high level. Despite his team's lackluster performance all those years, Hawkins played each contest full bore. After spending 1974 with the Cleveland Browns, he ended his 104-game NFL career with 261 receptions and 4,764 yards.

Once he hung up his helmet with the dangling chin strap for the last time, Ben devoted a number of years to coaching. "I coached for five years at Arizona State. Then I went with the Eagles, followed by the USFL San Antonio Gunslingers, where I was on the staff with my old Eagles teammate, Bill Bradley. Then I went with the Oklahoma Outlaws, where I was reunited with my old coach, Frank Kush. After I finished my coaching career, I got involved in the trucking industry, where I spent 10 years. These days, I'm kind of taking it easy."

These days, Ben Hawkins calls Belmar, New Jersey, his home. He lives there with his wife, Mary, and their two children, Ben and Nichole. Young Ben is following in his dad's footsteps—or pass patterns, as the case may be. He's a wide receiver at Moravian College in Bethlehem. Daughter Nichole is also an athlete who stars for her high school basketball team.

BUILDING UP TO THE GAME

Philadelphia was hoping for a quick turnaround from its 2-12 disaster in 1968. Though they didn't land O.J. Simpson in the '68 draft, the Eagles bagged a promising consolation prize in Purdue's Leroy Keyes. Most football pundits considered Keyes the nation's second finest collegian. Jerry Williams was Philly's brand new coach and Pete Retzlaff the franchise's brand new GM. The receiving corps had been "beefed up" with the acquisition of 5-foot-10, 175-pound Harold Jackson from L.A.

In the second game of the '69 season, Philadelphia was prepping for Pittsburgh, their cross-state rival. The Steelers had been the team's archrival since the inception of the Philadelphia franchise in the early '30s. As longtime announcer, Tom Brookshier's sidekick, and ex-New York Giant Pat Summerall sums up the rivalry, "The Eagles and the

Steelers were perennially the two toughest teams in the league. I mean physically tough. Sometimes it seemed like those guys were more focused on punishing you than beating you. I don't mean dirty. I just mean rock 'em, sock 'em football. You'd come away bruised and battered after those games. The Steelers had Ernie Stautner and the Eagles had Chuck Bednarik, 'Wildman' Willey, Pete Pihos, and a bunch of other guys who hit you so hard you didn't stop aching till the following Friday. That's if you were lucky enough to stop aching at all. So when Philly and Pittsburgh teed it up against each other, it was always a slugfest."

The "in those days" Summerall references started skidding to a stop by 1967. That was the year the two traditional rivals went their separate ways—the Eagles to the Capitol Division and the Steelers to the Century Division. Together, the Capitol and Century Divisions housed the reshuffled Eastern Conference of the NFL. At this point in 1969, both the Birds and the Steelers were frantically rebuilding. The Birds' program, as history records, fell substantially short of the Steelers'. Chuck Noll became the new Steelers coach in '69 (but only after Penn State coach Joe Paterno turned down the offer). Joe Green and L.C. Greenwood, who became two Steel Curtain mainstays of the '70s, were rookies for the black and gold that year. With a new coach and new blood like Mean Joe and L.C., Pittsburgh, much like Philadelphia, was hopeful for a resurrection into respectability.

The Steelers had started their season off with a win over the Lions. Meanwhile, the Eagles had lost a close one to the powerhouse Browns. The old fires of rivalry still flamed between Pitt and Philly and both teams needed wins to make a statement.

THE GAME OF MY LIFE
SEPTEMBER 28, 1969

Ben Hawkins: "As I remember it, we fell behind in the game. Cleveland had beaten us in a tough one 27-20 the week before. Of course, that was no disgrace. The Browns went on to win their division and made it all the way to the NFL championship game. [The Browns ran away with the Century Division in '69. Then they lost to Minnesota's Purple People Eaters and Joe Kapp, who went on to lose to KC in Super Bowl IV.]

"We had come off a bad year in 1968. [Actually, '68 was a butt-ugly year for the Birds, who finished dead last in the Capitol Division at 2-12.] We believed we were a lot better team than we had showed the year before and we felt we had strengthened the team in '69 when we brought Harold Jackson over from L.A. Harold was a great receiver. So we went into that Pittsburgh game with a lot of confidence, and at that point, we felt we were very much in contention.

"I think Pittsburgh had won their opener the week before. [The Steelers had upset the Detroit Lions.] Anyway, in this game, the Steelers jumped on top. But then we really came on. I can't give you any reason why we were so hot and why I was so hot that day. The Steelers had Paul Martha in the defensive backfield. He was a pretty solid DB and we weren't exploiting any particular guy or any particular weakness. The Steelers also had L.C. Greenwood and Mean Joe Green rushing our quarterback. But Norm Snead was throwing the ball great. [The Eagles QB had a superb day—22-30, 318, no interceptions.] The ball just kept coming my way and I kept catching it. It was that simple. It was just one of those days when everything clicked for us on offense. I think we scored another TD on a pass that day, probably to Harold Jackson. [Ben is correct—all five of the Birds' TDs came via the aerial route from Snead passes.] We had a couple of good running backs [Tom Woodeshick and Leroy Keyes], too, but it was one of those days you can't really explain, where everything that Snead threw up we ran under and caught.

"It was a great feeling coming back and turning that game around. We turned things around in the first half and we could just feel that was it. The game was ours. We took the lead into the locker room. I think I caught those four TD passes in a row, and I caught two or three of them in the first half to put us ahead at halftime. [Actually, Sam Baker wedged a 35-yard field goal between two Ben Hawkins first-half TD catches: the first of which was good for 26 yards, the second for 28 yards.]

"Then in the third quarter, I think I caught one or two more TD passes. [In the third quarter, Ben scored on two consecutive 15-yard strikes.] After that, Pittsburgh made a little run at us, but then we scored another TD—the one I think Harold [Jackson] caught. [Snead hit Harold on a 56-yard strike.] But the game was never in doubt.

"What a day! The details start to fade a bit over time, but not the feeling. How can any receiver not remember a day like that? Four touchdown passes—that's a dream for any receiver. And on that particular day, my dream came true."

WRAP

Ben's heroics took center stage in front of 60,658 Steel City fans who watched helplessly as the Birds quickly gobbled up Pittsburgh's 13-point first-quarter advantage. The Steelers had blasted out of the gate undeterred, scoring three successive times before the Eagles arrived at the party.

When the Snead-to-Hawkins show got underway, the game turned around. Behind Snead's imposing aerial attack in the second quarter, Philadelphia zoomed ahead 17-14. The Eagles burst out of the locker room after the first half with their momentum still intact. Two straight 15-yard scoring strikes to Hawkins stretched the lead out comfortably. Pittsburgh retaliated with a 3-yard Don Hoad scoring plunge and another Mingo field goal. However, Snead found another TD target in Harold Jackson. Sam Baker added a second field goal to pad a resounding 41-27 Philly victory.

Ben tied Joe Carter for the Eagles record for most TDs in a single game that day. Carter caught four six-pointers against the Cincinnati Reds on November 6, 1934. (Eagles end Swede Hanson also caught three for scores in the 64-0 shellacking that day. Given that the Eagles themselves had been shutout the three preceding games, the Birds' victory was so mind-blowing to Cincinnati that the Reds withdrew from the NFL immediately following the loss. The St. Louis Gunners replaced them.)

Since Ben's record-setting day in 1969, Irving Fryar has added his name to the Hawkins-Carter feat. Fryar assaulted the Miami Dolphins' defense for four scoring catches on October 20, 1996.

On the Eagles all-time receiving list, Ben Hawkins ranks 12th in number of receptions, seventh in most career receiving yardage, and eighth in career TDs. Ben's ranking in career TDs would sink from eighth to 10th sans that incredible September 28, 1969, performance.

"HOW WELL DO YOU KNOW YOUR BIRDS?" ANSWER
d) Pete Retzlaff (He wins with 24. Mike Quick is second with 21.)

Chapter 10

BILL BRADLEY

"SO, WHAT WAS THE GAME OF YOUR LIFE?"

Bill Bradley: "Playing ball in Philly was a terrific period in my life. I loved the Philly fans, and I had great teammates in Philly, too. I was fortunate. I had the opportunity to be a part of pro football in an era that was kind of unique. Things were starting to change in pro football when I first came up. When I think of the crew of veterans the Eagles had when I first came to Philadelphia, I'm amazed at the careers they had. Do you realize some of those old vets played college in an era when football players still wore leather helmets? That's how much the game changed in a short period of time. Salaries went up and the popularity of the game took off, and basically everything changed. But some of those guys who played in the old days were real characters, real interesting guys. They were also great teammates who took me under their wing and taught me a lot about the game.

"Now, getting back to the most memorable game, the game of my life, I'd have to say it was the first game I actually got into as a defender. We were playing against Dallas. Up until that Dallas game, the only thing I had been doing was returning kicks, punting, and holding for the place kicker. But in that game, I got in with the defensive unit. To do so, I had to do, well, a little negotiating. Anyway, it turned out to be a bigger thrill than I imagined, so I'll go with that game as the game of my life as an Eagle."

Bill Bradley holds down both the first-place and the second-place ranking in the Philadelphia Eagle record book for most interceptions in a single season. The 11 picks he snagged in 1971 are more than any other Eagle ever recorded. The nine he nabbed the following year tie him with Don "The Blade" Burroughs for second place on the same list. In terms of career interceptions as a Bird, Bill Bradley and Eric Allen share the top spot with 34.

Born on January 24, 1947, Bill Bradley is a native Texan. He went on to stardom with the University of Texas before being drafted by Philadelphia and heading east. He is remembered as a gifted interception artist, a precision punter, a superb holder for placekickers, and a reliable punt returner. Fans loved Bradley's hard-nosed style as well as the little something extra he saved for contests against Philadelphia's favorite gridiron nemesis, the Dallas Cowboys—the team that plays the Penguin to the Eagles' Batman.

HOW WELL DO YOU KNOW YOUR BIRDS?

Which player on the following list returned more career punt returns than any other Eagle in history? (Extra Credit: can you pick the all-time top five? Extra Extra Credit: can you place those top five in their proper order?)

a) Brian Mitchell   b) Bill Bradley
c) Wally Henry   d) John Sciarra
e) Larry Marshall   f) Tommy McDonald
g) Reno Mahe   h) Ernie Steele
i) Vai Sikahema   j) Timmy Brown

MEET BILL BRADLEY

William Calvin Bradley grew up in Palestine, Texas, where his father had become a sort of local hero. "They named a field after my dad—called it Joe Bradley Field," Bill explains. "My dad was a baseball coach in Palestine for 27 years. He was pretty revered in those parts of the state because of all the kids he worked with in sports. I'm still proud every time I see that field. My dad was my coach as a kid. He coached me in baseball and football. I used to go to his baseball camps when I was growing up, and he'd wind up using me as the guinea pig. You know, he'd make me be the one to show the kids how to slide and those kinds of things."

Bill learned his lessons well. He was an All-America quarterback at Palestine High, taking his team to the 1965 state title. He then moved on to a standout college career. "I played lots of baseball as a high school kid. Actually, I was drafted out of high school in the fifth round by the Detroit Tigers," Bill recalls. "But I opted for college when I got a scholarship to the University of Texas. I was the first one to go to college, the first generation in the family. So it was a proud day for me and all of us the day I made the decision to go on to college."

Bill was a gridiron star at the University of Texas. In his senior year, his Longhorns squad was ranked No. 3 in the nation. "We were a really great team," Bill reminisces. "The year after I graduated, Texas was ranked No. 1 in the nation. They were a powerful squad. Anyway, one day a few years after they won that title, I was talking to James Street, the guy who quarterbacked the national championship team. I asked James if he thought any other college team he'd ever seen could have beat them. James thought for a minute and said, 'The only team I ever saw that might have been better than us was the '68 Texas team.' I thought that was a pretty impressive tribute. Anyway, we did have a great Longhorns squad my senior season."

Indeed, with a record of 9-1-1, coach Darrell Royal's '68 Texas team was no slouch. Bill Bradley was one of the tri-captains on that Longhorns squad, which tied for the Southwest Conference championship. They earned a No. 3 ranking in the final Associated Press poll and a No. 5 ranking in the season-ending United Press International poll after topping Tennessee 36-13 in the Cotton Bowl.

Bill was the Longhorns QB for his first two years at Texas. (Those were his sophomore and junior years: freshmen were ineligible to play back then, when institutions of higher learning tenuously clung to the fading pretense that academics superseded sports in the institution's hierarchy.) After two games his senior year, however, Bill lost the starting quarterback role; he moved over to receiver for about five games, and then finished the season as a defensive back. "I kept changing positions all season. The only thing I did as a constant that year was to punt," Bill recalls. "You know how they listed me on the scouting reports? 'Punter/Player'!"

Regardless of position, Bill Bradley proved he was a solid athlete. When he slid over to his new role as defensive back, he did so with élan. He established a still-standing UT single-game record with four interceptions in the Longhorns' 35-14 win over Texas A&M. That record is not only a Longhorns standard, but also a Southwest Conference mark.

Following his collegiate career, the 5-foot-11, 190-pound competitor was selected to play in the 1969 Hula Bowl, the Coaches All-America Game, and the College All-Star Game. At graduation, the University of Texas awarded him their 1968 D.H. Byrd Leadership Award. (Byrd was a Texas oilman alumnus who—and here's a rare bit of trivia—owned the building leased to the Texas School Book Depository while Lee Harvey Oswald worked there.)

The Eagles picked Bill Bradley in the third round of the '69 draft. His arrival in the Quaker City coincided with one of the Eagles' more flurried transition eras. Jerry Williams was the Birds' new coach. Williams had been part of Buck Shaw's coaching staff on the 1960 Eagles championship team. He was replacing Joe Kuharich, whose blight on the Philly legacy and image is surpassed only by the city's 1844 Nativist riots (a.k.a., the prayer or Bible riots) and *The Gong Show*. OK, maybe *The Gong Show* reference is cruel. Suffice it to say, naming a more unpopular Philly coach than Joe Kuharich is a challenge.

As a rook, Bradley assumed the punting and kick returning chores. His sure hands also made him a skilled holder for the placekicker, a gridiron skill that is undervalued except by head coaches and guys who kick for a living. As a position player however, he made only rare appearances (but when he did … well, more on that later).

"My second season, I was hurt," the ex-Eagle states. "In the preseason, I hurt my right knee. I came back and did the punting again four weeks later, but I needed another knee operation after the season. They didn't have arthroscopic surgery in those days, so I basically missed my whole second season."

The Eagles finished at 3-10-1 in 1970. The following season, Steve Preece, one of the two starting safeties from the '70 squad, was gone. Ron Medved, the other starter in 1970, lost his safety position as the Eagles introduced a new safety tandem of Bill Bradley and Leroy Keyes.

Bill Bradley would retain the right safety position (as it was called then) through the '76 season. As for coach Jerry Williams, he was ousted after three games—and three losses—in '71. Philly fan-favorite Ed Khayat replaced Williams and the Eagles rebounded, finishing with a 6-7-1 record good enough for a third-place finish. Bill Bradley had become the Birds' premier player. The Eagles' No. 28 was the only Bird named

All-Pro in '71—the first of three such consecutive honors. He also made the first of four consecutive trips to the Pro Bowl.

Mike McCormack came to town in 1973 to pilot the squad. When Big Mike was ousted after a 4-10 season in '75, Dick Vermeil took charge. Bradley played one year under Vermeil's aegis before he was shuttled off to the St. Louis Cardinals. He performed one season for the Redbirds and called it quits.

"After my playing career, I ended up coaching," Bill explains. "In my 22 years of coaching, my teams had winning records 15 times. I broke into coaching with the USFL's San Antonio Gunslingers in '83. I was a combination defensive backs coach and personnel assistant. Then I moved on to the USFL's Memphis Showboats, followed by the University of Texas. Eventually I ended up coaching in Canada, but I also coached in the CFL for the San Antonio Texans and Sacramento Gold Miners and in the World League for the San Antonio Riders. I've been everywhere."

In recent times, Bradley was the defensive backs coach for the NFL's Buffalo Bills (1998-2000) and the New York Jets (2001-2003). Currently, he's the defensive coordinator for Baylor University. Bill and his wife, Susan, have two children, Matthew and Carissa.

BUILDING UP TO THE GAME

Mirroring the happenings in most of the country during the Vietnam era, the Eagles franchise was in turmoil. About a month or so before Bryan Adams bought his first real six-string at the five-and-dime in the summer of '69, the Eagles franchise was sold. On May 1, owner Jerry Wolman, a real estate magnate in Washington, D.C., unloaded the franchise he had bought five years earlier for $5.5 million on Leonard Tose. Trucking magnate Tose forked up $16.1 million for the pleasure. Former All-Pro Eagle Pete Retzlaff, who became the general manager, and Jerry Williams, one of Retzlaff's charges when Williams coached the 1960 NFL champion Eagles, were brought on board to steer the Eagles in the right direction.

The dissolution of the Eagles started slowly in 1967, when the Birds fell from a 9-5-1, second-place 1966 finish to 6-7-1. (This earned them second place in the weak Capitol Division. Nevertheless, they finished a couple time zones behind the 9-5 Dallas Cowboys.) By 1968, Philadelphia had slipped to 2-12, which cemented them solidly in the basement. Cries of "Joe must go" rang through Franklin Field as fans directed their frustrations at Joe Kuharich. So inept were the Iggles in the fans' eyes that the Birds couldn't even lose when they had to. In the legendary O.J. Simpson Bowl, the next-to-last game of the season, Philadelphia "trounced" perennial doormat New Orleans (who ended at 4-9-1) 29-17. That was Philly's highest point total of the year. The win sent O.J. to Buffalo. After the season, future Hall of Famer Mike Ditka proclaimed he would never play for Joe Kuharich again.

So Joe did indeed go. He was paid $49,000 a year over the next 10 years *not* to show up. Pete Retzlaff engineered a series of trades with the L.A. Rams. Perennial All-Pro tackle Bob Brown and Izzy Lang left for the West Coast and a cadre of eight mostly forgettables came to Philly in exchange. The unforgettable in the deal was wide receiver Harold Jackson.

The season started poorly. Cleveland bested the Birds 27-20 in the opener. The Eagles came out on top in their second game against the Steelers before losing successively to Dallas and the Baltimore Colts. Philadelphia headed into Dallas in week No. 5 as a heavy underdog. In front of 71,509 Texans, the Eagles took the field. Do not expect a glorious upset here. Do expect that one Texan had a day he never forgot.

THE GAME OF MY LIFE
OCTOBER 19, 1969

Bill Bradley: "I always saved a little extra for the Cowboys when we played. Being from Texas and playing for Texas, naturally the Cowboys had talked to me when I was in college. They told me they were going to draft me in the second round. Well, that round came and went for me. Dallas chose Richmond Flowers. Then in the third round, the Eagles picked me up. So I always had something to prove when we played the Cowboys.

"We were playing the game in the Cotton Bowl. That was exciting for me, going back to Texas and making my third appearance. When I was at Texas, we played SMU and Oklahoma at the Cotton Bowl. Then as a senior, we played and beat Tennessee in the Cotton Bowl game.

"I was just a rookie that year, just learning my way. I wasn't starting yet. I was doing all the punting and holding for the placekicker. I returned kicks, too—punts and kickoffs. But I wasn't playing much. I hadn't gotten to play with the defensive unit all season at that point. As it turns out, we were getting thumped pretty good by Dallas. Craig Morton was the starting QB for the Cowboys. I can't remember how many TDs he threw that day [he threw five], but the game was pretty much decided pretty early.

"So I started bugging our coaches, Jimmy Carr and Joe Moss, to put me in. I was telling them they should put me in to avoid risking injury to one of the starters. That was in the third quarter. I didn't get in. Then the fourth quarter, I kept it up. Funny, I've been coaching all these years now, so I know what it was like for them listening to me. Looking back, I guess I was a little out of line. For whatever reason, though, finally they gave in and sent me in for Joe Scarpati. Turns out I wasn't the only rookie that went in. Dallas had Roger Staubach in for Morton. Remember, Staubach had played for Navy and was drafted in 1964, but because he had his service commitment, he didn't come into the NFL till 1969 [as a 27-year-old rookie]. And Mike Ditka had left the Eagles the year before and landed with Dallas. But the thing was, Ditka and Staubach had never really worked together.

"I had studied films of Dallas. We were at the point in the game where Dallas was just trying to kill the clock. I knew from the films that if Dallas saw a blitz coming, they adjusted. They would audible to a play where the quarterback gets rid of the ball fast. Staubach saw we were blitzing and checked off the play at the line of scrimmage. Ditka didn't hear it, though. I knew the spot they'd be throwing to, so I went to that spot. It was supposed to be just a quick slant to the tight end. That's where Staubach threw it, but I was the only one there. Then I managed to cut back, use some blocks, and go all the way.

"So I hate to say it, but that's the game I remember best, just because it was the first time I actually got to play in a game for the Eagles aside from special teams play. I ended up scoring on a 56-yard touchdown interception.

"I'll tell you something else funny about that play. You know, I was hardly the fastest guy out there on the field! I think the Dallas flanker, Robert Hayes [who at one point held the title, "The World's Fastest Human"] was in the far end zone when I intercepted the ball. He took off after me and, by the time I reached the other end zone, he had caught up to me.

"So the game didn't end up good for the Eagles, but I had a chance to show the coaches what I could do. I also had a chance to show something to Dallas and to do something big in front of the fans from my own state. That made it a pretty special day."

WRAP

Bill's heroics didn't result in his immediately cracking the starting squad. The following week he was relegated to punting, kick returning, and holding duties once more. Two years later, however, he became a rock-solid performer who closed out his career atop the Eagles' all-time list for career interceptions and most interceptions in a single year.

"HOW WELL DO YOU KNOW YOUR BIRDS?" ANSWER
d) Wally Henry (He tops the list with 148.)
EXTRA/EXTRA EXTRA CREDIT:
1) Wally Henry (148)
2) Tie: Brian Mitchell and John Sciarra (117)
4) Bill Bradley (111)
5) Larry Marshall (104)

Chapter 11

JOHN OUTLAW

"SO, WHAT WAS THE GAME OF YOUR LIFE?"

John Outlaw: "Of course I remember the Miracle of the Meadowlands. Who wouldn't? That was a great game, and I really think it set the Eagles up for the success that was about to come—the success that eventually led the Eagles to their first Super Bowl appearance. But the Meadowlands game was played near the end of my career. As for myself, I didn't play much in that particular game. I think the games that stick out for me were the first games I played for the Eagles. I had just finished up four years in New England. When Chuck Fairbanks came on as the Patriots coach, I wasn't part of his plan. He started what he called 'a youth movement' and I wasn't a part of it. That seemed strange to me. I was only 26 years old at the time! Luckily, John Mazur, who coached me at the Patriots, happened to be on the Eagles staff just when New England was letting me go. John brought me over to Philadelphia. But I came in while the season was in progress, so I didn't feel fully comfortable for a while. That's why it was such a thrill for me to grab a big interception against the Jets. That's the game I remember: the Jets game. That game made me a full-fledged Eagle. That's the game I'd pick as the game of my life as an Eagle."

John Outlaw came to Philadelphia in 1973 after a four-year stint with the Boston Patriots (the AFL precursor to the NFL New England Pats) and the New England Patriots. He spent six years in the Birds' defensive backfield before hanging up his No. 20 jersey forever. His most productive Eagles season came in 1975, when he picked off five passes—a figure that equalled all-time Eagles interception leader Bill Bradley for team best for the season.

John terms his Philly tenure "the great days of my career." Smiles John, "I loved the city of Philadelphia. I loved the people there." He started his Eagles career during coach Mike McCormack's regime and retired with the franchise on the Dick Vermeil upswing that led to the team's first Super Bowl appearance in 1980. His retirement came on the heels of the Eagles' first postseason appearance since 1960 (excluding Philadelphia's two appearances in the ludicrous Miami Playoff Bowls in '61 and '66).

John tallied 13 interceptions as an Eagle. The 5-foot-10, 180-pound athlete was a solid performer and hard-nosed defender.

HOW WELL DO YOU KNOW YOUR BIRDS?

Shades of Van Brocklin/Waterfield, the Eagles sent not one but two quarterbacks to the Pro Bowl one season. What was the year and who were the QBs? (Pick two from the following list.)

a) Sonny Jurgensen

b) Norm Van Brocklin

c) Adrian Burke

d) Mike Boryla

e) Roman Gabriel

f) Pete Liske

g) Bobby Thomason

h) King Hill

i) Norm Snead

j) Jack Concannon

k) Ron Jaworski

MEET JOHN OUTLAW

John L. Outlaw was born January 8, 1945, in Clarksdale, Mississippi, where he attended Higgins High School. After graduation, he headed off to Jackson State University, where his performances on the gridiron attracted enough attention to land him a 10th-round selection by the AFL's Boston Patriots in 1968. John made the Pat squad, but saw limited action as a rookie. By his third year, he had worked his way up to a starting role. In his first season as a starter, he registered three interceptions. By that time, the Boston Patriots had joined the NFL and changed their handle to the New England Patriots.

"In 1973, Chuck Fairbanks came over to the Patriots from the University of Oklahoma," John Outlaw recalls. "He had lots of success at Oklahoma." (Fairbanks became the Sooners coach in 1967 after then-head coach Jim Mackenzie died suddenly. Fairbanks led Oklahoma to three Big Eight titles. However, three months after Fairbanks was named Patriots head coach, Oklahoma was mandated to forfeit nine games from their '72 campaign because of recruiting violations involving altered transcripts. Oklahoma was prohibited from appearing in Bowl games for two years. Fairbanks denied knowledge of the altered transcripts.)

"Unfortunately, I didn't fit into Chuck Fairbanks' plans," John Outlaw muses. "But John Mazur happened to be on the Eagles staff under Mike McCormack. John had coached me at Boston. So I was fortunate to find a place to start over."

John not only started over in Philadelphia, but remained in the City of Brotherly Love, becoming an Eagles fixture for the next six years. "I remember being at a party one night, right?" John recalls. "It was after the '79 season. Some of my teammates and Dick Vermeil were there. That's when I told Dick that I was calling it quits. Dick was saddened, but he cared for his people. Dick understood that when your time as a player is up, you know it. ... That's how I felt. My time as a player was up. I had no regrets. I got a lot of mileage out of my pro football career. It was time to move on."

And move on is just what John Outlaw did. His post-NFL career has been very fruitful. The first post he filled was that of defensive coordinator at North Carolina Central University. He held that position for 11 seasons. For two of those years, he simultaneously served as director for the National Youth Sports Program. His next career move, however, was a departure from the norm. John joined his friend, Bernie Bickerstaff, who was filling the dual positions of president and general manager of the National Basketball Association's Denver Nuggets. "Bernie told me there was a spot open in community relations," John reports. "So for four years, I worked in community relations before migrating over to the basketball side of the organization. In reality, my duties those years represented kind of a mixed bag. For instance, I did some scouting during the NCAA tournaments. I served as a scout for a year and a half as I worked my way up to director of college scouting."

John Outlaw spent two years with the Washington Wizards as assistant coach and advance scout before moving over to the Charlotte Hornets. At this writing, he is heading into his third season as an assistant coach with the Charlotte Bobcats. Outlaw cautions, "Look, my function is far more administrative than strategic. I'm not an Xs and Os type of coach. During a game, you'll find me sitting in the row behind the bench. Basically, my duty is to watch the shot clock and maintain the hustle charts. The hustle chart records things like long rebounds, loose balls, steals, blocked shots. Mostly, I keep everybody aware of what's going on. Another important function I fill is to evaluate college talent and prepare for the NBA draft."

Another unusual bullet on the John Outlaw CV is his work with the U.S. Department of Education, where he consults on safe and drug-free schools.

John's son, J.J., is an undrafted free agent with the Eagles. J.J. starred as a Villanova gridder for four years. In a stellar career, he earned all-conference honors three times and hauled in 199 passes for 2,326 yards and 16 touchdowns.

"We didn't think that J.J. would get drafted," the senior Outlaw confesses. "That doesn't mean we weren't hoping! Actually, we hoped that some team would invite him to a camp and give him a chance. As it turns out, the Eagles were the team that invited him. At the beginning of the seventh round, the Eagles telephoned J.J. and indicated they would sign him as a free agent if he didn't get drafted. They kept good on that promise."

BUILDING UP TO THE GAME

The lowly Birds of the early '70s were struggling to regain respectability when John Outlaw came to town. At the start of the '73 season, the franchise had engineered a number of front-office shake-ups. Owner Leonard Tose accepted GM Pete Retzlaff's resignation and Mike McCormack replaced Ed Khayat as head coach. The team had acquired Roman Gabriel from the L.A. Rams to spearhead their hoped-for, on-field resurgence. Gabriel came at a high price. Philadelphia surrendered Harold Jackson, Tony Baker, and three draft picks for the Rams star. However, the move paid off. After a pathetic 2-11-1 showing in 1972 when John Reaves and Pete Liske shared the QB position, Gabriel lent leadership and stability to a formerly anemic offense. He also added potency. Gabriel finished the '73 season as the NFL leader in pass attempts (460), pass completions (270), passing yardage (3,219), and TD passes (23). The 6-foot-5 Gabriel was tossing the ball to a tall group of targets: Harold Carmichael (6-foot-8), Charle Young (6-foot-4), and Don Zimmerman (6-foot-3). Collectively, they were known as the Fire High Gang. The entire squad responded to the team's offensive success and the Eagles scrapped their way to a respectable 5-8-1 record.

The team hadn't jelled at first. They followed a woeful 1-5 preseason with an opening-game loss. They managed a tie with the Giants before losing the next two to the Redskins and Bills. They didn't bag their first win until game five against the St. Louis Cardinals. From then on, they played .500 ball. In fact, they played .500 ball right on through the following season, which they finished at 7-7.

As game 13 of the '73 season approached, the Birds had nowhere to go in terms of playoff berths, but they had plenty to prove. So did recent arrival Johnny Outlaw. "I was happy when I arrived," Outlaw recollects. "This team had a good, veteran feel and they had a lot of confidence in themselves. I was accepted right away, even though I arrived in midseason. But that's a tough time to arrive for a player to break in with a group of guys he doesn't know. I wasn't at training camp and I still had to prove myself to the guys. They didn't know who I was or what John Outlaw was all about. By the time the Jets game came along, I was playing more and more. I was getting used to the system in Philadelphia. I was just looking for a chance to show everybody that I could contribute."

When that chance came, John Outlaw didn't blow it.

THE GAME OF MY LIFE
DECEMBER 9, 1973

John Outlaw: "We got off to a bad start in the Jets game. NY scored two TDs in the first few minutes. [After six minutes, the Jets zoomed out to a 14-0 advantage.] Their running back, Emerson Boozer, scored both TDs. [Boozer was a big Jets star in the Super Bowl that Joe Namath 'guaranteed' a victory in a few years earlier.] I think that was it, though, for the Jets offense. We shut them down after those early TDs.

"We were lucky that day. We didn't have to face Namath. Joe was supposed to be the starter, but when game time rolled around, Al Woodall, a big QB [6-foot-5, 205 pounds], trotted out onto the field. Woodall played the whole game, so the Jets were not at their maximum strength.

"Anyway, after those two early Jets TDs, we launched a comeback. We marched down the field. Don Zimmerman caught a short TD pass to culminate the drive. That put us back in the contest. Then the Jets kicked a field goal before Harold Carmichael caught a long pass [a 67-yarder] for a second TD. Harold got behind their defensive back [Earlie Thomas]. Harold was a youngster at the time. He ran the final few yards backwards. A few years later when Dick Vermeil took over, Dick made Harold and others stop that kind of display. I was glad to see that. Anyway, Harold's TD closed the gap to 17-14.

"That was the score when my big moment as an Eagle arrived. I got lucky and positioned myself properly on one of Woodall's passes. The pass came right to me and the field started to clear when I took off downfield. I ended up taking it home. [John scored on a 45-yard interception return.] My interception put us up and we held on for the win. But most important for me personally was that the interception and return made me feel I had contributed. I had done something that helped give the team a win. I was officially an Eagle."

WRAP

December 9, 1973, was a big day for the NFL—a record-setting day for "stay aways." Eagles fans led the pack. Battling the double whammy of playing the contest in an ugly, steady, Philly drizzle and playing a meaningless game with no playoff implications, 31,333 ticket holders (47 percent of the anticipated crowd) stayed away from Veterans Stadium. That year marked the NFL's first experience after the hated full blackout had been abolished. Until 1973, home games in NFL cities were blacked out, i.e., not aired in the hometown. (Modern-day fans might be surprised to learn that even the 1960 Eagles NFL championship tilt with Green Bay was blacked out in the Quaker City. Philadelphians evacuated the City of Brotherly Love en masse and headed for New York to catch the contest on the tube.)

The Eagles offense proved a potent force once more in this battle. QB Gabriel connected on 14 of 25 tosses for 215 yards and two TDs. Carmichael alone accounted for 146 of those yards, thanks to his five snares of Gabriel's flares.

One thing John Outlaw failed to mention was that, after his game-winning interception return, the Eagles had a big scare. Emerson Boozer, who ran wild all day long (in addition to his two TDs, Boozer rolled up 160 yards rushing) rumbled 52 yards before he was caught and grounded at the Eagles' 11. The Eagles D stiffened and forced the Jets to settle for a field goal, which brought NY within a point at 24-23. But that was all she wrote for both teams. That's how the game ended, and John Outlaw had a game to remember forever.

"HOW WELL DO YOU KNOW YOUR BIRDS?" ANSWER
c) Adrian Burke and g) Bobby Thomason. Both went to the Pro Bowl in the year 1955.

Chapter 12

VINCE PAPALE

"SO, WHAT WAS THE GAME OF YOUR LIFE?"

Vince Papale: "Every game I ever played as a Philadelphia Eagle was the game of my life! When you dream your entire life about playing with the Eagles and then one day you find yourself putting that uniform and helmet on, well, there's no such thing as a forgettable game or forgettable moment. I think they captured that spirit in *Invincible*, the movie about me. Didn't they do a great job? I was thrilled with that project, beginning to end. And for the most part, I'd have to say it was pretty factual. They did kind of lump some things together, like combining a few different plays into one for the sake of time and drama, but the movie showed how magical the whole experience was. As for the game of my life, well, certainly the first time I walked onto that Vet Stadium turf as a Philadelphia Eagle is something I'll never forget. When I ran through that tunnel after they announced, 'And now, the rest of the Philadelphia Eagles ... ,' well, I still get goose bumps. But the game of my life would probably be the '78 game against the Redskins."

Vince Papale was an Eagles' season-ticket holder in the Vet's wild and woolly 700 section, which was both famous and infamous. (What does infamous mean? As Chevy Chase explained it to Martin Short in Three Amigos*: "Oh, Dusty, in-famous is when you're MORE than famous. This man El Guapo, he's not just famous, he's IN-famous." So, too, were the ticket* *holders in the 700 section.) Vince had attended Interboro High School, where he starred in track and earned a track and field scholarship to St. Joseph's College (now a university).*

After college, he taught high school for a few years. In 1976, he participated in an open tryout for the Eagles and, against all odds, made the squad. His story, which parallels Philly's revered Rocky *saga (at least the first* Rocky *movie—Vince never came close to ending the Cold War by battering a Russian), has been immortalized on the silver screen. Vince's story,* Invincible, *was released in 2006 and was tops at the nation's box office its first two weeks. Today, Vince still lives in the Philly area and still bleeds Eagle green.*

HOW WELL DO YOU KNOW YOUR BIRDS?

Pick the only two Eagles quarterbacks who have recorded three 400-yard plus passing games:

a) Tommy Thompson   b) Norm Van Brocklin
c) Randal Cunningham   d) Adrian Burke
e) Bobby Thomason   f) Sonny Jurgensen
g) Davey O'Brien   h) Mike Boryla
i) Roman Gabriel

MEET VINCE PAPALE

Vincent Francis Papale, born February 9, 1946, grew up in the Philly area. He was a three-sport letterman at Interboro High, starring in football, basketball, and track. His forte was the pole vault. He still holds the school record for the outdoor pole vault at Interboro, where his exploits earned him a full scholarship to St. Joe's for track and field. Vince captained the Hawks track team his senior year and won the school's coveted Most Outstanding Senior Athlete in 1968. At St. Joe's, Vince retains the school record for the indoor pole vault.

Vince Papale watches the action from the Eagles sideline during a preseason game against the Pittsburgh Steelers in 1977.
George Gojkovich/Getty Images

After his collegiate days (when he earned an MS in Marketing/ Management Science), Vince taught business education in the Interboro school district for about six years. He also served as the high school's head track coach and assistant football coach. "I was in great shape," Vince reminisces. "I worked out with the kids all the time—running, sprinting, putting myself through all their drills. I was actually in training myself. I planned to try out for the decathlon in the Olympics. But the fact is, all that hard work helped me realize my dream to play professional football."

Vince followed that dream in 1974. He made a leap of faith, relinquished his teaching position, and tried out for the Philadelphia Bell in the newly formed World Football League. He landed on his feet, hooking on with the Bell as a wide receiver. The 6-foot-2, 195-pound athlete played in the ill-fated league till it folded in 1975. Then, as the legions who have watched *Invincible* know, Dick Vermeil debuted in Philly, replacing the shell-shocked Mike McCormack. Vermeil announced an open tryout for the Birds. Vince heard the call, tried out, and made the squad—the sole survivor. In making the team, he set an NFL record: at 30 years of age, Vince was the oldest rookie ever to suit up in the NFL.

He remained an Eagle for the next four years, cementing his legend as Philly's Rocky in the flesh.

During his Eagles stint, Vince was voted captain of special teams. In 1978, he was voted Philadelphia Eagle Man of the Year in recognition of his many charitable activities. A shoulder injury ended his career in '79. He has remained in his beloved Philly ever since, pursuing a multifaceted career path. Vince was a Quaker City sportscaster for eight years before shifting careers to the commercial mortgage industry. Today, he is a marketing executive and special projects director for Sallie Mae.

As for the story behind how and why *Invincible* came to happen, Vince Papale explains, "ESPN did a piece on the 25th anniversary of *Rocky* and they chose my story for the show. They figured my story paralleled Rocky's—an older Philly guy getting a chance of a lifetime and beating the odds. The piece was only a few minutes long, but the response was amazing! Hollywood got interested and the phone started ringing. What a thrill! I'll be honest, I have loved every minute of the whole project. It's such an honor for me personally, and getting to know people like Mark Wahlberg [who played Vince] and the whole crew has been a highlight of my life. They were great with my family and kids.

"I thought Mark was a perfect choice to play me. Mark and I were both poor kids growing up. We both suffered our knocks, but found a way to turn things around and get on the good path. Mark and I have become friends. He just called me yesterday—invited me to his Super Bowl party. My family and I will be down there with him watching the Super Bowl and rooting for the Eagles, hopefully. [Unfortunately, New Orleans dashed those hopes, so not this year, Vince.] And Mark is a fine athlete. It's funny. Do you know what the hardest thing for Mark to do was? It was catching a football with the helmet and all the pads on. He had a helluva time adjusting to that. He had never played organized football wearing pads before. The other problem he had was getting down into a three-point stance. But aside from those little things, he did a super job."

Vince is married to the former Janet Cantwell, who is portrayed by Elizabeth Banks in the movie. The couple holds a singular distinction in the Keystone State. Janet is a former member of the U.S. Olympic gymnastics team. Both she and Vince have individually been inducted into the Pennsylvania Athletic Hall of Fame. No other married couple can stake that claim.

Vince and Janet live in Cherry Hill, New Jersey, with their children, Gabriella and Vincent.

BUILDING UP TO THE GAME

Dick Vermeil arrived in Philly in 1976, where he inherited a team that (well, let's put it this way) didn't quite measure up to the bar Vermeil set in terms of commitment, hard work, and dedication. His Birds struggled. They finished a disappointing fourth place in Vermeil's frosh and soph campaigns. However, in their second season, the team showed signs of life. The '77 season ended with a mini-flourish as the Birds swept and smoked two Big Apple squads. They whipped the Giants 17-14 before closing the season with a 27-0 demolition of the Jets. Philly-fan skepticism persisted. Only 19,241 fans showed up for the finale in cold, miserable, Christmas-season weather. The Iggles faithful set the dubious NFL standard that day for no-shows as a whopping 43,013 chose to stay home.

Nonetheless, with a new 16-game regular-season format, the '78 season opened unceremoniously as the Birds dropped their first two games. "Same old Eagles" was the cry of the defeat-weary hometown fans. However, these were *not* the same old Eagles. They rolled out three straight wins before dropping one to the Pats and evening their record at four wins and four losses. The Eagles found themselves at a crossroads as the undefeated Washington Redskins prepared to assault the Vet.

THE GAME OF MY LIFE
OCTOBER 15, 1978

Vince Papale: "This was my second year as an Eagle. I was comfortable in my role on special teams at that point. I remember that October Sunday from beginning to end. The team ate its pregame breakfast together at the Stadium Hilton like we always did before home games. Afterwards, Dennis Franks and I hopped into my Datsun 260Z. Wow, was that car hot! Everybody in town knew it! It was Kelly green with the Eagles logo painted on it. My friend, Bill Palo, did a beautiful job painting that car. Bill is still doing that kind of work around Philly. He's the guy who owns all the Executive Auto Bodys. We were blasting down Columbia Avenue, going like 80 mph. [To Philly cops who are reading this, I'm no attorney, but I hope the statute of limitations pertains here.] We had that first Santana album blasting and we were screaming, getting pumped for the game.

"We worked our way up Pattison Avenue and we drove by that park with the golf course not far from the stadium. We saw two kids playing football. Then I noticed that one of the kids was wearing an Eagles No. 83 jersey—my jersey! So Dennis and I stopped and walked over to the kids. I asked them if we could have a catch with them. The kids said yes. Then after a couple of minutes, the kid wearing my jersey number said to me, 'You run like my idol, Vince Papale!' He didn't recognize me! I was unshaved and wearing a hood. So Dennis and I told them who we were, and they were worried we'd miss the game! It was hours before game time, so we told them not to worry. We signed our autographs and took off, but when we were leaving, I told the kid, 'I'm gonna make a special play for you today.'

"The game was close—a real tough one. We were really hitting them all over the field. We caused a lot of turnovers. [The Birds forced six altogether—four on fumbles and two on interceptions.] Our defense got us a lead. [Deac Sanders intercepted an errant Redskins pass and returned it 19 yards for a score.] I think Nick Mike-Mayer kicked a field goal too. [He did—a 29-yarder.] I'm not sure what our other score was. [Wilbert Montgomery ran one in from 12 yards out.]

"Anyway, it came down to a punt at the end of the game. Our punter was having a nightmare game. He was a guy named Mike Michel, who had replaced Rick Engles. I think Mike got one punt off clean, but then he bobbled the snap on another and had a whiff on another one. Mike had a concussion, and on that whiff, it was windy and the wind kind of blew the ball away from him as he was swinging his leg. Anyway, we were backed up on our 10 and had to punt. The Redskins called timeout to try to rattle Mike. Mike and I were good friends at the time, and I kept telling him, 'Just keep visualizing those beautiful punts you were getting off in practice today.'

"If you saw *Invincible*, this was the white-knuckle play they showed. Dennis Franks actually did teach me that little tip. When a guy is down in a three-point stance, if he's coming forward to get you, his knuckles can't help getting white. If he's not coming at you, the knuckles won't be white. When you're in a three-point stance, it's almost impossible to look up anyway. The Washington guys were all talking trash to shake up the punter, saying they were coming in to get him. So I looked at the knuckles on the Washington guys. I could see they weren't coming in, so I called an audible at the line. All our guys were basically supposed to slide to the right to protect me so I could get downfield. They did, and I got off flying downfield. It was like a movie: everything, all the crowd noise, went silent. The only thing I could see in front of me was the Washington punt returner, Tony Green, who was the league's top return man. I just ripped into him full speed and the ball popped out. I was in great position to pick it up and take it in, but Billy Campfield jumped on top of it. Basically, that was the game. All we had to do was run the clock out.

"That footage of Dennis Franks and me hugging each other and celebrating, the footage they show in the movie—that was after that play. The stadium erupted. You know, there's a photo of Dennis and me snapped at that moment in Canton. A guy at the *Wilmington News Journal* snapped a shot, and it's now hanging in the Hall of Fame.

"What a day! What a group of guys on that Eagles team! We were so close, all of us—I'm the godfather of Dennis Franks' kids—and after games, we'd usually get together at someone's house or we'd all meet at

Brownie's Pub on Second Street. Those years with the Eagles were like a dream come true."

WRAP

There's a moving, virtually cinematic prologue to the game of Vince Papale's life.

"Last year," Vince relates, "I was in a restaurant somewhere around 17th and Sansom. A guy came up to me and said, 'Vince, you won't recognize me, but I'm the kid that you had the catch with in the park all those years ago.' Naturally, I didn't recognize him. He was all grown up now. But he remembered too much about what happened that day to have been duping me. It was him. What a thrill that was to see this kid all these years later."

A passing scene in the movie is based on that incident. Mark Wahlberg, as Vince, is driving pensively through the streets of Philly. He looks to his left as he passes a group of kids playing football. He stops as a kid walks in front of his car and hustles back to the game. The boy is wearing a No. 83 jersey. The kid in that scene happens to be Vince's real-life son, Vincent. What goes round comes round.

"HOW WELL DO YOU KNOW YOUR BIRDS?" ANSWER
c) Randal Cunningham and f) Sonny Jurgensen

Chapter 13

FRANK LeMASTER

"SO, WHAT WAS THE GAME OF YOUR LIFE?"

Frank LeMaster: "When I started in '74, things weren't going too well in Philly. That sure changed when Dick Vermeil came in '76. I was fortunate to participate and contribute to those great years of Eagles football. ... I can point to so many great games, important games, and personally gratifying games. In my second season, I had a great game in the season finale at Washington. We crushed them 26-3. That was Mike McCormack's final game as Eagles coach. I think I had two interceptions off Joe Theisman that day and ran one of them back 89 yards for a TD. [That play marked the longest interception-return for a TD by a non-DB in Eagles history.] But I think for pure—I guess you'd call it maybe disbelief or seeing something I've never seen on a football field—I'd have to pick the Miracle of the Meadowlands. That's one of the most famous games of all time, and I was on the field and in the thick of the action when it all took place."

Frank LeMaster was a key building block of the Eagles defense in the late '70s and early '80s. Frank exemplified the kind of dogged pursuit and determination that characterized the Philly teams of the Dick Vermeil era. LeMaster was a fourth-round draft choice in 1974 who earned a starting left linebacker slot his sophomore season. He kept that starting slot, along with jersey No. 55, through eight consecutive campaigns. Frank kicked off his career at the end of a bleak Eagles era and called it quits after the absurdity of the strike-ruined 1982 season, which also saw the departure of coach Dick Vermeil. LeMaster left a legacy of commitment and dedication that immortalized him with the fans.

HOW WELL DO YOU KNOW YOUR BIRDS?

Ken Houston of the Oilers (1971) and Jim Kearney of the Chiefs (1972) hold the NFL record for most interceptions returned for TDs in one season. They share that record with an Eagle. Each member of this elite trio returned four interceptions in a single season for touchdowns. Who is the Eagle that shares the record?

a) Troy Vincent   b) Russ Craft
c) Jerry Norton   d) Bill Bradley
e) Eric Allen   f) Don Burroughs
g) Wes Hopkins   h) Bobby Taylor

MEET FRANK LeMASTER

Frank Preston LeMaster, born March 12, 1952, migrated north to the Quaker City from Kentucky in 1974. "I remember when I got drafted by the Eagles," Frank recounts. "I was just happy to be drafted. Someone asked me what I knew about the Eagles, and I said all I knew about them was that I liked their helmets."

A graduate of the University of Kentucky, Frank didn't see much playing time as a rookie except on special teams. He also backed starter Steve Zabel and learned the NFL linebacking trade. The next year, the 6-foot-2, 232-pound competitor won the starting job. Together with Bill Bergey and John Bunting, Frank completed the tough-hitting, aggressive linebacker trio that formed the heart of the team's tenacious defense for six seasons.

He posted his most impressive stats in his first season as a starter. That's the year he picked off four passes and returned them for a total of 134 yards. Possibly overshadowed by the much-acclaimed Bill Bergey,

---

A determined Frank LeMaster (No. 55) pursues a Pittsburgh opponent.
AP Images

Frank was overlooked for Pro Bowl honors most of his career. Interestingly, after Bergey retired, Frank was finally accorded his due in 1981 and selected to the Pro Bowl along with fellow LB Jerry Robinson, nose tackle Charlie Johson, CB Roynell Young, and TO Jerry Sizemore. He played but one more season, calling it quits after the 1982 campaign. Frank LeMaster is remembered as someone who practiced his craft with the kind of blue-collar, ready-to-rumble verve that endears gridders to Philly fans.

Currently, Frank lives and works in the Philadelphia area. He has forsaken his native Bluegrass State, but nonetheless earns his living working in the field of grass, so to speak. He's the vice president of sales for FieldTurf, which makes artificial turf for sports and various other usages. "That turf on the Vet was terrible," Frank notes. "I can't imagine how many injuries that caused and how much it increased the possibility of injury."

BUILDING UP TO THE GAME

Heading into the fray at the Meadowlands on November 19, 1978, the Eagles found themselves in third place in the NFC East behind the Dallas Cowboys and Washington. The Giants languished in fourth. Both the Eagles and Giants had playoff hopes, especially since this was the first 16-game NFL season ever. Each knew they would have to settle for a wild-card berth, however, because the powerful Dallas Cowboys had amassed a solid lead in the NFC East. Given the similarity of the combatants' records—the Eagles at 6-5 and Giants at 5-6—the day's outcome had critical playoff implications since the first tiebreaker for a wild-card spot included head-to-head records. Thus far in '78, the Giants and Eagles had not squared off. The return match was scheduled for the final game of the season.

The Giants were returning home after a three-game losing streak on the road. A win against the favored Eagles would give the New Yorkers a much-needed shot of rhythm and blues and keep their hopes of a playoff spot alive. In contrast, the Eagles were riding a two-game win "streak." (Streak? Philly grabbed for any straw it could in those days.) Both opponents were trying desperately to extricate themselves from the long, seemingly interminable era of mediocrity they were mired in. The Giants and Eagles had not played in the postseason since 1963 and 1960, respectively, so the faithful from both cities were clamoring for a morsel of success.

THE GAME OF MY LIFE
NOVEMBR 22, 1978

Frank LeMaster: "That game didn't start out positively for us. We were both hungry teams, but I believe we were always hungrier than any opponent. That was a hallmark of the Vermeil era and style—hunger and conditioning. He drove us hard physically and we were always more than ready physically for anyone. As for our poor start, the Giants scored and we fell behind. I think Pisarcik threw a TD pass or two before we scored. When Wilbert scored for us, we had that weird play on the extra point. [Eagles kicker Nick Mike-Mayer was injured after a high snap aborted the possibility of a boot and he unceremoniously tried to pass the ball, Garo Yepremian-style.] Then the game rolled along and we scored a second TD. Again, we missed the extra point. [After Mike Hogan scored on a short plunge, Eagles holder Mike Sciarra fumbled the snap, and incredibly, Mike Michel, who suddenly found himself both kicker and punter, missed the Eagles' second PAT of the day.]

"The Giants had also kicked a field goal, so we were down 17-12 with the end of the game closing in on us. We had the ball trying to score near the end of the game, and Jaws [Eagles QB Ron Jaworski] threw an interception. [Giants' rookie DB Odis McKinney's first NFL interception came with less than two minutes left and sent NY fans scurrying to the exits early to soak in the scenic, exquisite ambience that cloaks the New Jersey Turnpike. It was a sub-par day for Jaws, who was picked off three times and completed 15 of 31 passes for 164 yards.]

"That's when the game got 'famous.' The Giants had the ball and ran a play on first down. They had brought over Larry Csonka, who had played in the other football league that folded, and O.J. Anderson. Both those guys were great backs, but when they got to the Giants, they weren't the same backs they had once been. Pisarcik took a kneel-down on second down, but Bill Bergey and I and the rest of the Eagles line jumped the center. We tried to push the center [Jim Clack] back into the QB. The Giants didn't like that. There was a lot of chatter out there on the field. We were frustrated and figured we should have won the game.

"Then came the third-down play, third-and-2. We all rushed the line, the whole unit. Pisarcik tried to hand the ball off. I can see it yet, like it's in slow motion. The ball bounced and went right to Herm Edwards, who ran it in 26 yards for a score. I have never seen such a shocker! What a feeling!

"I know the Giants had some dissension and a lot of repercussions from that play. They fired their offensive coordinator, Bob Gibson, the next day. As for the Eagles, I think that game made us solid. It made us believe we could always win no matter what the situation. The Miracle of the Meadowlands went a long way towards shaping the character of the squad that made it to the Super Bowl two years down the road."

WRAP

All kinds of lore have sprung up in the wake of the Miracle at the Meadowlands. The week before the game, some of the offensive players reportedly had complained about the team's assistant coaches, specifically targeting Gibson. When Gibson saw the Eagles' surge that pushed the Giants' center back into the QB on the second-down play, the coach didn't want to expose his young QB to injury. He called the 65 power-up play for Csonka. In some reports, the Giants were stupefied by the decision in the huddle. Csonka refused the ball. The center hurried the snap because the game clock was winding down. Pisarcik's fingers got jammed on the snap ...

Who knows which elements are true and which are myths? The fact remains: the Miracle at the Meadowlands was a key episode in shaping the Super Bowl squad of 1980, and it was the game of Frank LeMaster's bountiful life as a Philadelphia Eagle.

"HOW WELL DO YOU KNOW YOUR BIRDS?" ANSWER
e) Eric Allen (He did it for the Birds in 1993.)

Chapter 14

WADE KEY

"SO, WHAT WAS THE GAME OF YOUR LIFE?"

Wade Key: "Probably the game that gave me the most pleasure was a Monday night game where we beat Dallas. I'm a Texas boy and we had lots of other Texas guys on that team, so beating Dallas in front of a national audience was special for all of us. I forget what year that game was played right now. As the years roll by, you know, the details start to fade a bit, but the game, I believe it was in '78 or '79 [the game took place on November 12, 1979], was one of those games that professional football players take with them long after they leave the playing field."

Wade Key, born October 14, 1946, was a little-known NAIA (National Association of Intercollegiate Athletics) All-American tight end at Southwest Texas State when the Philadelphia Eagles drafted him in round 13 of the 1969 draft. He reported to the Eagles training camp, made the squad, and was immediately shifted to offensive tackle. Eventually, the 6-foot-5, 245-pound athlete was moved to offensive guard, where he remained for the rest of his 10-year NFL tenure, spent entirely with Philadelphia. Wade was a Philly standby, a guy who unceremoniously but proudly manned the mean trenches of the NFL scrimmage line for guts rather than glory. His work ethic was outstanding, and the people of Philadelphia embraced him.

"It was intimidating for a small-town kid like me to come to the big city like Philly. I used to walk around staring straight up at all those big buildings

and I'd be amazed. But I found out the people in that town were wonderful. And you gotta love those Philly cheesesteaks! There's still nothing like them anywhere! Do me a favor, Bob. You tell all those fans back there how ol' Wade Key still appreciates every one of them. I'll never forget them. They were the greatest."

HOW WELL DO YOU KNOW YOUR BIRDS?

Which offensive tackle listed below played fewer than three Pro Bowls as an Eagle?

a) William Thomas
b) Bob Brown
c) Floyd Peters
d) Frank "Bucko" Kilroy
e) Jerry Sisemore

MEET WADE KEY

"I'm really just a small-town, country boy," Wade Allan Key acknowledges. "I was born in a little town in Texas on the outskirts of San Antonio. I played high school ball here and then went to a little college you probably never heard of called Southwest Texas State. After my junior year there, the Los Angeles Rams called me about drafting me. I kept telling them the same thing: I didn't want to be drafted. I had another year of college to finish and I wanted to finish it before thinking about playing professional football. So don't you know, the morning after draft day I got a phone call that the Philadelphia Eagles had drafted me in the 13th round. That set me to thinking. I thought, 'You know, I might get injured if I play another collegiate year.' You never know about those kinds of things. Then I'd never have a chance to play pro ball. So with the bonus the Eagles offered and the salary they were throwing out, I decided to take my chances and turn pro."

The bonuses and salaries Wade is talking about are hardly gaudy compared to football's current, giddy, out-of-hand stipends. Wade Key's bonus amounted to $8,600. His first contract was for $17,500, but that was enough to woo him to Philly. Quarterbacks these days make that much for each snap they take.

"First thing they did when I got to camp was to make me an offensive tackle," Wade recalls. "That was in 1970. That's the position I played my first three years. Then Mike McCormack came on as head coach and moved me over to offensive guard. I stayed there for the rest of my career."

As for the way his career ended, No. 72 admittedly did not have as tidy an exit as he would have liked.

"I guess you'd have to say it ended on a misunderstanding," Wade notes a bit sadly. (Any malingering grapes of wrath seem withered on the vine at this point.) "I had surgery in February after my last season. Of course, I didn't know it was my last season when I had the surgery. They removed a huge calcium deposit from my hamstring. I wasn't supposed to play again till September. I was still rehabilitating when summer camp opened. As it turned out, during the preseason, a lot of linemen got hurt and [head coach] Dick Vermeil asked me to go in. He wanted to protect [QB] Ron Jaworski. I went in and played for the sake of the team, but I played hurt. Then when September rolled around, I was waived. I was confused, to say the least. At the time, the whole thing was passed off as a misunderstanding, but it hurt."

After his playing career, Wade became a coach. Now a resident of Hondo, Texas, he ended up coaching the high school team near his hometown. "I've really enjoyed coaching all these years," Wade offers. "But I'm calling it quits now so I can spend more time on my ranch and just enjoying life."

BUILDING UP TO THE GAME

Dick Vermeil arrived in Philadelphia in the bicentennial year of 1976. His teams had losing records in his first two campaigns. Then, in 1978, the Eagles managed a winning season, a feat they had not accomplished since 1966. They also fought their way to a playoff appearance, which they had not done since 1960. Notwithstanding those achievements, the fans of Philadelphia weren't sold on the team's credentials. Iggles fans remained loyal but skeptical.

The Eagles started the '79 season like a house afire. They won six of their first even games before hitting the skids and dropping three in a row. So when the Eagles winged down to Dallas, E-A-G-L-E-S fans were pessimistic—especially since it was a Monday night contest.

"We had lots of Texas boys on that Eagles team," Wade recalls. "We were fully confident we could match up with anyone. So even though we had lost three in a row, we went down to Dallas that night expecting to win."

THE GAME OF MY LIFE
NOVEMBER 12, 1979

Wade Key: "The game didn't start out too promising for us. We found ourselves down right off the bat [wrong sport, but you get the metaphor]. The game had just gotten started when Roger [Dallas quarterback Roger Staubach] tossed a long TD pass. [Jolly Roger connected with wide receiver Drew Hill on a 47-yard scoring strike 61 seconds into the match.] But those Vermeil teams had no quit in them. We came right back. I think one of our linebackers, Jerry Robinson, recovered a Dallas fumble. Then Jaws [Eagles QB Ron Jaworski] tossed a [22-yard] TD to Harold Carmichael and we were tied.

"Then we got another break, followed by a great individual effort. Randy Logan recovered another Dallas fumble for us. The offense didn't advance the ball too much, and Coach Vermeil was forced to give Tony Franklin a shot at a long field goal. It was a 59-yarder and Tony nailed it! At the time, I think that was the second-longest field goal in NFL history. And we were on our way to what I also seem to recall would be the Eagles' first victory ever at Texas Stadium.

"Oh yeah, before Tony kicked that ball—and let me remind you that Tony was another good ol' Texas boy—Charlie Smith caught a TD pass. That TD was set up by another fumble recovery. [Eagles linebacker Frank LeMaster recovered a Dallas fumble on a punt.] Charlie's TD was the go-ahead score for us. The guy who threw the TD pass was not Jaws, though. It was John Walton, our backup QB. Jaws had gotten hurt … and missed most of the second quarter. Jaws did come back in the second half. He was a tough guy, no doubt about it. It took a lot to keep him off the playing field. The same thing happened to Roger Staubach. Roger was knocked out of the game in the first half for a while, but he came back in the second half, too.

"We had Dallas down 17-7 at half. Then, with Jaws back at the helm in the second half, we struck first. Jaworski hit Harold Carmichael for another score, but with Roger leading the way, Dallas never stopped coming at you. Staubach found Tony Hill with another long pass [a 75-yarder] for a score, and the next thing we knew, Dallas was back in the game. Roger found Billy Joe Dupree, their big tight end, for a 5-yard score, and suddenly we were in a real dogfight. When we got the ball back, we set up Wilbert Montgomery and ol' Wilbert, he ran one in from about 40 yards out [it was a 37-yarder]. That wrapped up the game for us. I helped open the hole Wilbert scooted through. The whole Eagles offensive line had an exceptional night against a tough Dallas D that night.

"Yep, beating Dallas was a sweet victory. Like I say, I had a good game. I wouldn't call it my personal best game, but hey, any time you travel to Dallas for a *Monday Night Football* game, you pretty much have to bring your A game or you might as well stay home. The A game is what we brought that night. I was proud, as always, to be a Philadelphia Eagle."

WRAP

With their victory over Dallas, the Eagles launched another winning streak, this time a four-gamer. They closed the season out by winning five of their final six.

The game of Wade Key's life proved to be a big night for all kinds of personal achievements. Receiver Harold Carmichael caught a pass in his 107th consecutive game. Linebacker Jerry Robinson made his first start, and it was a memorable one. On one superb play, he jarred the ball loose from the great Cowboys running back Anthony Dorsett before pouncing cat-like on the ball himself. Eagles running back Wilbert Montgomery became the first Eagles back ever to log consecutive 1,000-yard rushing seasons. Against Dallas, Montgomery toted the ball 25 times for 126 yards. Among the receiving corps, Carmichael caught four for 69 yards and Charlie Smith pulled in four for 54 yards and a TD. Meanwhile, in the trenches, Dallas defenders would have had a tougher time breaking by Wade Key than Jimmy Johnson has passing a comb through his hair.

"HOW WELL DO YOU KNOW YOUR BIRDS?" ANSWER
e) Jerry Sisemore (He was selected to two Pro Bowls as offensive tackle. All others on the list were selected to three.)

Chapter 15

CLAUDE HUMPHREY

"SO, WHAT WAS THE GAME OF YOUR LIFE?"

Claude Humphrey: "That's a tough question to answer if you're talking about games I played during my time with the Eagles. We were always winning! It was great coming to Philadelphia and being in Philadelphia those years because we had such powerful teams. If you asked me the same question about Atlanta games, it would be easier to pick. … We hardly won any. So all the games in Philly were memorable. But let's see. I think the game I remember most was the playoff win against the Vikings after the 1980 season. That was our game. We dominated and we played real Eagles football from beginning to end.

Claude Humphrey came to Philly after an illustrious career with the Atlanta Falcons. Claude was drafted No. 1 by the Falcons in 1969 and roared to instant stardom in the NFL. After earning All-Pro or All-NFL honors in eight of the following 10 seasons, Claude was shipped to Philly for two fourth-round draft choices. "I basically asked to be traded, and Philly was where I wanted to go," Claude says today. He arrived in Philly during some dominant Eagles years. Claude played only three years in the Quaker City, after which he retired. However, his level of play did not diminish in Philly. In three of the past four years, Claude Humphrey has been a finalist for induction into the Pro Football Hall of Fame.

HOW WELL DO YOU KNOW YOUR BIRDS?

Which Eagles quarterback has completed the most passes in postseason play?

a) Ron Jaworski   b) Donovan McNabb
c) Randall Cunningham   d) Norm Van Brocklin
e) Tommy Thompson

MEET CLAUDE HUMPHREY

Claude B. Humphrey was a Tennessee kid, born June 29, 1944, and raised in Memphis, where he starred on the gridiron for Lester High School. After high school, he forged a national reputation at Tennessee State. The lowly Falcons drafted him in the first round of the '69 draft (Claude was the third pick overall), and Atlanta was not disappointed. Claude immediately blossomed into a perennial All-Pro. Claude's personal contributions notwithstanding, the Falcons managed only two winning seasons in his decade-long stint in the capital of the New South. By and by, he tired of losing and finally, after his 10th season in an Atlanta uniform, Claude Humphrey asked to be traded.

How good was Claude Humphrey in Atlanta? The 6-foot-4, 252-pound athlete's Atlanta career included twice being named All-Pro (1972-1973), thrice being selected Second Team All-Pro (1969, 1974, and 1977), twice being honored All-NFC (1970-1971) and once being named Second Team All-NFC. In 1976, Humphrey unofficially recorded a career-high 15 quarterback sacks. In addition, he was named to the Pro Bowl six times in the course of his 10 years in Atlanta. He played 127 games as a Falcon and still ranks as the Falcons' career sack leader with 62.5, good for 510 yards.

"When I asked to be traded, I didn't want to wind up just anywhere," Claude confesses. "Philadelphia was the place I wanted to go specifically. Why? 'Cause coach Dick Vermeil was in Philadelphia. So was defensive coordinator Marion Campbell—the old Swamp Fox. Marion had been my head coach and my defensive coordinator at Atlanta. I thought it would be helpful to me personally to reunite with Marion at that point in my career."

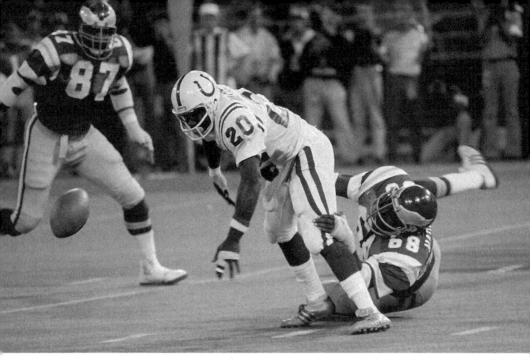

Claude Humphrey (No. 87) watches as teammate Dennis Harrison (No. 68) forces Colts halfback Joe Washington to fumble. *AP Images*

Claude didn't wait for a trade. He left the Falcons after four games in the '78 season and didn't play the remainder of the season. The hiatus didn't deter him when he started the '79 season as an Eagle. In his first season with the Eagles, No. 87 finished second in sacks and led the Birds with 31 quarterback hurries. In 1980, he registered a team-leading 14.5 sacks.

"I felt like I was personally part of the team here in Philly," Claude avers. "I felt the same way about the city of Philadelphia. What terrific people Philly has! It was the whole mix here in Philly—the fans, my teammates, the coaching staff, and the Vermeil philosophy. Football in Philadelphia is intense. The fans really care. It wasn't like that in Atlanta. The way Philadelphia looked at its football team was the way I always felt football should be. I guess you could call it camaraderie between the team and the fans. And then there was the camaraderie within the team itself. Getting a chance to play in Philadelphia and getting a chance to meet the Philly fans was something I'll never forget. Like I said, the fans were amazing. People in Atlanta didn't even recognize me when I was out in public. Here in Philadelphia, the fans knew me wherever I went. They used to bring us hoagies into the locker room. We never got treated like that in Atlanta.

"As for talent on the football team, I thought there were a few other teams in the league at the time that had as much talent as the Eagles. Some might even have had more. But the Eagles excelled because of our rare camaraderie and because of the belief we had in ourselves. I mean, at Atlanta we just didn't win enough. It's not that we didn't have talent. It's just that it always seemed to be too much of an individual thing in Atlanta. That wasn't the Vermeil system. It was all about team success."

The statistics support Claude's sentiments. During the defensive end's three seasons with the Eagles, they rolled to 33 victories. In his 10 seasons at Atlanta, the Falcons won but 50 times.

"The best thing that ever happened to me was coming to Philadelphia," Claude sums up. "I played in all those playoff games and got a chance to play in a Super Bowl. That wasn't going to happen in Atlanta. Plus, the people I met here were all wonderful—everyone from great teammates to a fine coaching staff and super fans. Yeah, I loved my days in Philly."

BUILDING UP TO THE GAME

In 1979, the juggernaut that Dick Vermeil had spliced and diced together matured into a force to be reckoned with. The Birds won the wild-card playoff before getting upset by the Tampa Bay Buccaneers 24-17 in the division championship. Vermeil had substantially bolstered the '79 team with the addition of Jerry Robinson, Petey Perot, Tony Franklin, Leroy Harris, and, of course, sack-master Claude Humphrey. Meanwhile, No. 1 draft choice Roynell Young moved directly into a starting slot.

The Eagles' '80 edition soared off right from the get-go. They trounced three consecutive opponents 27-6, 42-7, and 35-3 before submitting to the St. Louis Cardinals. The Birds recovered quickly to rattle off victories in the next eight contests, which gave them a comfortable divisional lead. Still, they didn't nail down the division title till the final game of the regular season.

By 1980, the Birds had gained respectability throughout the football world. Quarterback Ron Jaworski, wide receiver Harold Carmichael, nose tackle Charlie Johnson, and safety Randy Logan were all selected as NFC starters in the Pro Bowl. Charlie Johnson repeated as an All-Pro.

Jaworski was the leading NFC passer with 257 completions in 451 passes for 3.529 yards, 27 touchdowns, and 12 interceptions.

Dick Vermeil had his charges pumped up for the postseason. The Eagles resolved to take the postseason one game at a time. They entered the fray a confident bunch, experienced and wiser from the events of the preceding year, when Tampa Bay stopped their march in the opening round.

THE GAME OF MY LIFE
JANUARY 3, 1981

Claude Humphrey: "We fell behind early by a couple of touchdowns. I forget how they scored the first one. [It was a 30-yard scoring strike from Tommy Kramer to Sammy White.] I think they scored the second on a short plunge. [Running back Ted Brown took it in from the 1-yard line.] We were behind 14-0 near the end of the first half, but I honestly don't think there was any sense of panic. Then, near the end of the half, we had a long march [Ron Jaworski engineered an 85-yard scoring drive] and Ron Jaworski found Harold Carmichael for a score. That put us right back in the game before we went into the locker room.

"That second half, we came out to play! I think we scored a touchdown right out of the gate. ... Didn't Wilbert [Montgomery] run one in? [Yes, he did—No. 31 lugged the ball in from 8 yards out.] Then a weird thing happened. Minnesota sacked Jaws and we were behind 16-14. But we came right back, and Wilbert ran another one in for us. Our defense shut the Vikings down for good at that point. I don't think we allowed Minnesota another point. We started playing aggressive and forcing turnovers. I think on Minnesota's final four drives, we ended each drive with an interception or by forcing a fumble and recovering it. ...

"I had a good game against Minnesota in the playoffs, but I played better games that year. The gratifying thing about playing well against the Vikings is that I was going up against Ron Yary, one of the best offensive linemen in the business. Ron was a perennial All-Pro and apparently, before I got to Philly, he pretty much dominated the Eagles, but for some reason I seemed to match up successfully with him. Recording a few sacks and hurries by getting past Ron Yary gave me a lot of personal satisfaction. As I said, I did turn in some more dominant performances in other games in terms of statistics. I think I had four sacks against New Orleans and three against the Raiders, but as far as personal satisfaction goes and as far as being part of a great defensive unit that was performing at its peak, it's tough to beat the playoff win over Minnesota.

"And the fans that day! I never played in an atmosphere that was so charged up. Those fans were so behind us that day. They were so into the game. The whole game long, I thought they were going to pour out of the stands and onto the field. Normally, we would have appreciated that, but the way our defense played that day, we didn't need the help!"

WRAP

The Eagles fielded a crushing defense in 1980, due in no small measure to the performance of Claude Humphrey. They limited the opposition to a miserly average of 22 points per game. Ten times that season they held opponents to fewer than 100 rushing yards. In the playoff tilt versus the Vikings, Minnesota led 14-7 at half (even though Tony Franklin had missed a 24-yard field goal that would have tightened the score to 14-10). All in all, the Vikings, under relentless Eagles pressure, turned the ball over 11 times, including eight turnovers within a remarkable 23-play stretch at the end of the game. The Eagles defense completely took over the game in the second half when they snagged five interceptions and snuffed out every hint of a Vikings resurgence.

"HOW WELL DO YOU KNOW YOUR BIRDS?" ANSWER
b) Donovan McNabb

Chapter 16

DICK VERMEIL

"SO, WHAT WAS THE GAME OF YOUR LIFE?"

Dick Vermeil: "Well, of course everyone knows what I'm gonna say. It was the big win over Dallas 20-7 back in 1981—the game that sent us to the Super Bowl. Sure, there were lots of other big games that I'll always remember, but this was the one we were working toward for five years. This was the team we were gunning for all that time during the Eagles' climb. We set our sights on Dallas for years and now here they were. We had them in our sights."

Dick Vermeil brought his enthusiasm into Philadelphia from the West Coast in 1976. His work ethic and insistence on total dedication and effort from his charges endeared him to the Philly faithful. After a tearful 1982 resignation from his Eagles head coaching position, he eschewed the coaching ranks for a decade and a half. To the surprise of many, he resurfaced with the St. Louis Rams and retired again immediately after winning Super Bowl XXXIV. This time, his hiatus was brief. A year later, he took the reins of the Kansas City Chiefs for five years before quitting for good. Although Dick worked in a number of locales after quitting the Eagles head coaching position, he never left Philadelphia. He has called the Philadelphia region his home since his 1976 arrival.

HOW WELL DO YOU KNOW YOUR BIRDS?

How many of the coaches listed below did not win Coach of the Year honors?

a) Greasy Neale   b) Buck Shaw
c) Dick Vermeil   d) Ray Rhodes
e) Bert Bell   f) Andy Reid

MEET DICK VERMEIL

Richard Albert Vermeil was born in Calistoga, California, at the northern end of Napa Valley in the heart of San Francisco's wine country on October 30, 1936. Dick lettered in four sports at Calistoga High School and still found time to work in his dad's auto repair garage. He played football one season at Napa Junior College before moving on to San Jose State. He was backup QB for the Spartans his senior year. (In 2000, he was inducted into the San Jose State Hall of Fame.)

After college, Dick began coaching for San Jose's Del Mar High School. He followed with stints at Hillsdale High, San Mateo College, and Napa Junior College. He moved up to NCAA Division I when he joined Stanford from '65 to '68 under head coach John Ralston. Then, in 1969, he became the NFL's first-ever special teams coach for the Los Angeles Rams under George Allen. He took a hiatus in 1970 to serve as an assistant coach with UCLA. The following year he was back with the Rams, where he remained till he was named head coach at UCLA in 1974. In two seasons for the Bruins he recorded a 15-5-3 record. The Bruins' 9-2-1 slate in 1975 brought them their first Pac-8 championship in 10 years and a huge Rose Bowl win over an undefeated and No. 1-ranked Ohio State team.

Eagles owner Leonard Tose sought out the suddenly renowned UCLA mentor in 1976 and wooed him to Philadelphia to replace Eagles head coach Mike McCormack. Although the Eagles hadn't chalked up a winning season since '66, Vermeil led the Eagles to a playoff berth in his third year at the helm. He won NFC Coach of the Year honors in the process. In 1980, the Eagles went to Super Bowl XV and Dick was named NFL Coach of the Year for the first time.

Coach Dick Vermeil (center) attempts to gain his players' attention from Philadelphia sidelines during a 21-10 upset of the New England Patriots on August 27, 1977. *AP Images*

Following a 14-year coaching sabbatical, Vermeil returned as president of football operations and head coach of the St. Louis Rams in 1997. The St. Louis team had suffered through seven consecutive losing seasons. However, in '99, Dick guided the Rams to a 13-3 regular-season record and a 23-16 victory over Tennessee in Super Bowl XXXIV. St. Louis was dominant, containing opponents to 21 points or less in all 13 regular-season victories. Their average margin of victory was 22.9 points. Nineteen years after winning the NFL Coach of the Year honor with the '80 Philadelphia Eagles, Dick reprised the act with the Rams.

Eleven days after the Super Bowl victory, Dick announced his retirement from the Rams. Less than a year later, he re-upped as head coach, this time with the Kansas City Chiefs, where he called it quits for good in 2005. In his third year at the KC helm, Dick and the Chiefs made the playoffs with a 13-3 season. That season, he also became only the fourth NFL head coach in history to take three different teams to the playoffs. For those of you keeping score, the others include Chuck Knox (Rams, Bills, and Seahawks), Dan Reeves (Broncos, Giants, and Falcons), and Bill Parcells (Giants, Patriots, Jets, and Cowboys). He also joined Knox, Reeves, and Parcells as just the fourth coach in NFL history to record a 10-victory season with three different teams.

Currently, Vermeil works as an analyst with the NFL Network. He and his wife, Carol, have three children: Rick, Dave, and Nancy. The Vermeils live in Chester County, Pennsylvania.

BUILDING UP TO THE GAME

"When I came into the league, Dallas was the gold standard," Dick Vermeil asserts. "They had great teams every year. They were in our division and it was obvious to me that, to be successful, the Philadelphia Eagles would have to overtake the Cowboys. That's what I set out to do. We gained on them every year, but in 1980, we were ready.

"When we beat them in Dallas on a Monday night game in 1979, I knew that we were catching up. At that point, our whole team understood that we could play Dallas and beat them. We hadn't beaten Dallas for five years before then. [Even more disturbing, the Eagles hadn't beaten Dallas in Dallas since 1965.]

"When 1980 came, we played good, sound football all year. We beat Dallas at the Vet earlier in the season. We played them in the last game of the year in Dallas. As long as we didn't lose by 25 points or more, we would win our division. We fell back by 27 points or so and then came back. I never panicked. I knew we were a good football team and we beat them up in the second half.

"We won that [NFC divisional playoff] game against Minnesota, and the stage was set for the Cowboys. I wanted us to get a good week of practice in. It was cold in Philadelphia. We used to practice in the old JFK Stadium, which was miserable. So we went to Florida to practice. We had a really effective week. That was really my reason for going—the bad weather in Philly. I think I got the guys thinking that the Cowboys took us for granted. I sold our guys on that idea and it motivated them.

"When we came back up to Philly we were set for the Cowboys. Our guys were hungry and they believed in themselves."

THE GAME OF MY LIFE
JANUARY 11, 1981

Dick Vermeil: "We were ready. I could feel it in the locker room before the game. … I'll never forget when we came out of that tunnel onto the field. George Allen was standing there and he said to me, 'Dick, you guys are going to beat the hell out of them!' He could feel the intensity, too.

"As for big plays, the big play I remember right off the bat was the hit that John Bunting made. John smelled out a screen pass and just knocked the hell out of the ball carrier. Carl Hairston knocked the hell out of the lineman and the quarterback on the rush on the same play. Our guys were hitting them all over the field.

"Then, of course, there was Wilbert Montgomery's run. We had terrific, crisp blocking on that play. The line knew that was all you had to do for Wilbert—just give him an ounce of daylight and he'd be gone. That's what they did and that's what Wilbert did. He turned it into a score.

"The weather changed our game plan. … We wanted to throw more, but couldn't. We also wanted to run a lot of draw plays, but it was extremely windy that day and cold, and that changed our play calling.

"I had confidence the whole game—before the game—that it was our day. Our guys were not going to let this one get away. We knew we had caught Dallas and we all wanted to show the world we had."

WRAP

The Eagles' euphoria subsided two weeks later, when the Oakland Raiders thumped the Birds 27-10. In 1981, the Birds burst out to a 6-0 start. However, the rest of the way they managed only a 4-6 log. Their 10-6 seasonal mark earned them a wild-card slot. However, the Giants downed them 27-21 in front of 71,611 at the Vet to end the season. The following year, football was disrupted by a strike. The Eagles sank to 3-6, and Dick Vermeil, as he termed it, "burned out." He stepped down as Eagles head coach, and the Dick Vermeil era ended abruptly.

"HOW WELL DO YOU KNOW YOUR BIRDS?" ANSWER

One: e) Bert Bell (Yep, the only Eagles owner who ever coached the squad had a lifetime coaching mark of 10-44-5 for a .185 won-lost percentage, excluding ties. Tell that one to Jerry Jones. As for the rest of the coaches listed, *The Sporting News* gave Greasy Neale the award in 1948, UPI and AP both gave Buck Shaw the award in 1960, *The Sporting News* and *Pro Football Weekly* gave Dick Vermeil the award in 1979, the AP, *The Sporting News*, the Maxwell Club, and NFL Films gave Ray Rhodes the award in 1995; *The Sporting News*, the Maxwell Club, and *Football Digest* gave Andy Reid the award in 2000, and the AP, *The Sporting News*, the Maxwell Club, and *Pro Football Weekly* gave Andy Reid the award again in 2002.)

Chapter 17

MERRILL REESE

"SO, WHAT WAS THE GAME OF YOUR LIFE?"

Merrill Reese: "Bob, there were so many memorable games and they were memorable for so many reasons! I've listed several of my favorites in my book, *It's Gooooood!* But let's see, just off the top of my head ... January 11, 1981, pops up. It always does, and why shouldn't it? If I think of days when the belief and excitement in this town about the Philadelphia Eagles were at their peak, I don't know what days I would put ahead of this one. ... That's when we beat Dallas in the NFC championship game here.

"Some of the other contenders are: the Miracle at the Meadowlands in '78, when Herm Edwards ran the Pisarcik fumble in for a TD with less than 30 seconds to play; then there's the 99-yard pass play from Jaws [QB Ron Jaworski] to Mike Quick in '85 against Atlanta—that was the longest pass completion in Eagles history; and then, in the same vein, there's the second-longest Eagles pass play—that's when Randall Cunningham made a superhuman effort shedding Bruce Smith in the end zone. Bruce Smith, of all people, one of the greatest sack artists in NFL history! Smith was about to sack Randall, but Randall broke free and eventually somehow found Fred Barnett way downfield for a 95-yard score.

"I've seen so many big plays and so many big games over my years in the booth, like the '89 game when we beat the 'Skins 42-37. Their

119

back, Gerald Riggs, ran wild that day. He gained about 200 yards. Then, with a little over a minute left in the game and Washington ahead 37-35, Riggs ripped off a long run. It looked like a clincher, except that Eagles DB Al Harris stripped the ball and handed it to Wes Hopkins. Wes ran it 77 yards to the 4-yard line. Then Randall tossed his fifth TD of the day. What an incredible turnaround!

"But OK, getting back on track to answer your question, if I have to pick my one most memorable game, well, it just had to be that playoff against Dallas."

Since 1977, Merrill Reese has been the voice over the airwaves most associated with the Eagles. When Merrill talks, people listen. Merrill is a Philly guy through and through, as was Bill Campbell, the Voice of the Eagles in Merrill's youth. Merrill graduated from Overbrook High and went on to broadcast sports and music at Temple University. His professional broadcasting career, which kicked off in Pottstown, Pennsylvania, has never let him stray out of the Delaware Valley.

HOW WELL DO YOU KNOW YOUR BIRDS?

In 1939, the trio of Taylor Grant, Bob Hall, and Harry McTigue became the first official Eagles broadcast team. They broadcast Eagles games on WCAU, which continued as the Eagles flagship station till 1945. Since then, various other Philly radio stations have served in that capacity. Which of the following radio stations was *not* at one time or another an Eagles flagship radio station?

a) WIBG   b) WCAU
c) WIP   d) WOGL
e) WYSP   f) WPEN

MEET MERRILL REESE

Born in West Philadelphia, Merrill Reese was the son of a dentist. His mother was a kindergarten teacher smitten with the entertainment biz. She gently steered her child toward showbiz and her quest met with success. Merrill became a child star and a busy little beaver (not as busy, of course, as the bona fide Beaver, Jerry Mathers, but the Beav's not up to much these days). He managed to land a number of roles, particularly on local Philly TV. Of note, Merrill was a regular on Philly's *Sealtest Big Top*.

The future Voice of the Eagles was also the kid who yelled, "Hey kids, it's time for *M&M's Candy Carnival!*" on the show with the same name (duh). He appeared on *Six Gun Cinema* with Chuck Wagon Pete, whose real name was Pete Boyle—an easel-drawing artist whose son, Peter Boyle (a LaSalle College grad), really hit the big time. Yes, he's the same Peter Boyle who portrayed the monster in Mel Brooks' campy *Young Frankenstein* as well as the deadpan, cranky Frank Barone in the popular CBS sitcom *Everybody Loves Raymond*.

Young Merrill Reese also nabbed some bit parts in films shot in Philly. He appeared as an extra in Cecil B. DeMille's *Greatest Show on Earth*, which won the 1952 Oscar for Best Picture. During the filming, Merrill had a catch with Jimmy Stewart on the set. But as Merrill grew into adolescence, his acting opportunities dried up. "Since we didn't live in Hollywood where most of the opportunities were," he explains, "I just kind of got out of the acting thing. Not only that, the need for child actors is much greater than it is for teens."

Merrill went to Overbrook High School, which had gained notoriety a few years earlier when Wilt Chamberlain was a student. "I wanted to play basketball, even though I loved baseball and football so much," Merrill says, looking back. "Basketball ruled in my neighborhood. I played nonstop at Overbrook Park at the Lamberton schoolyard. But even in those days, Overbrook recruited players from all over the city. I tried out, but the tryouts were just a formality. The team was already picked. Three of the starters in my sophomore year went on to star in the NBA: Wali Jones, Walt Hazzard, and Wayne Hightower."

Merrill's dad died in his senior year at Overbrook. The future broadcaster didn't want to stray too far from home for college, so he enrolled in Temple as a communications major. Merrill joined Temple's radio station staff, WRTI. He started off as a disc jockey, playing 45-rpm records. The first sporting contest he announced was a Temple-Villanova baseball game at Villanova. He schlepped his 60-pound reel-to-reel tape recorder to the Main Line, set up extension chords along first base, recorded his play-by-play, and played it back later on the campus station. By the end of his freshman year, Merrill was named the station's sports director. He succeeded Tom Cardella, another guy who (eventually) made a career as a Philly broadcaster.

At a football pep rally as a Temple sophomore, Merrill was blown away by an Owls fullback who took the mike and had the audience howling. Merrill asked the guy if he'd like to tape a show with him. The fullback agreed, and *The Bill Cosby Show* was born.

The professional media world did not beat down Merrill's door once he graduated Temple. After tons of rejections, he managed to land his first broadcasting job covering high school basketball games in Pottstown for station WPAZ. There was a catch. The station made him go by the name Alan Reese. Apparently, a name like "Merrill" posed a threat in the pre-9/11 world. In any event, his assignments included covering a fire engine parade in Collegeville, reading death notices at a cemetery as organ music swelled in the background, and covering Little League baseball games.

He had some unusual experiences in those days. For instance, Little League baseball broadcasts were a must. What that means is that, since the station had the sponsor's check firmly in hand before the game was played, the show had to go on, rain or shine. "One time I called the station, saying the game was rained out," Merrill chuckles. "The station's powers-that-be insisted that 'the show must go on!'" And so it did. "I went back to the stands and invented a game, at-bat by at-bat!" (Phillies' broadcaster Harry Kalas had similar experiences that you can read about in my book, *More Than Beards, Bellies, and Biceps—the Story of the 1993 Philadelphia Phillies*.)

After almost a year, Merrill was lured away from WPAZ to WCBC in Levittown. "Big" money was the culprit. Isn't it always? Merrill made some pretty stiff salary demands. To his surprise, they were met—and then some. Merrill had asked for a salary of $100 a week. The station magnanimously upped the ante to $102.50 a week. It was too much for Merrilll to resist, so he set out for Levittown. In the ensuing years, Merrill's voice graced several Philly stations, including WWDB, WHAT, and WIP. In 1975, he ascended to sports director at WWDB.

In 1977, Merrill Reese replaced Al Pollard as the full-time color analyst for Eagles football on WIP. Pollard was stepping down because he needed to devote more time to his newly developed business. "I'll always believe they tapped me for the job because of a dinner I had with Ed Khayat in 1974," Merrill confides. "Eddie was a Detroit coach when the

Lions came to town in '74. He and I had dinner and he gave me the entire lowdown on everybody on the Lions. The next day, I received an emergency phone call asking me to fill in for Al Pollard because he was sick. I did, and I had a terrific day on the air because Ed had given me all that info the night before."

Since 1977 and without interruption, Merrill Reese has remained the Voice of the Philadelphia Eagles.

BUILDING UP TO THE GAME

"The Eagles had come so far!" exclaims Merrill Reese. "That's what made this day and this game so special. It was Philly's first championship game since the '60 Eagles took the NFL flag. That was exciting in itself, but there was the whole 'Dallas thing,' too.

"Everybody in Philly sort of has a 'Dallas thing.' It started almost as soon as the Cowboys joined the NFL in 1960. Coach Dick Vermeil himself admits that he used Dallas as a lightning rod for the team's emotion. Vermeil used to tell the teams in that era, 'Dallas is doing things better than anybody else in this league. That's the team we have to catch.' Vermeil told all his players that they had to work hard, and if they did, they were going to catch Dallas and beat Dallas.

"The Eagles team got off to a marvelous 11-1 start in '80. As the year rolled along, it just seemed like things were falling in place just as the coach predicted. It really seemed to all of us that this was truly the year we would overtake Dallas. ... Then Philadelphia went to Dallas to play the final regular-season game. Because of the playoff set-up, all Philadelphia had to do to clinch the NFC title was to avoid losing the game by more than 24 points. Well, Dallas ended up jumping out to a 35-10 lead! But then the Eagles battled back to whittle the final score down to 35-27. It was still an Eagles loss, but we did win the NFC title and the right to host the NFC title game.

"In the playoffs, the Eagles beat the Vikings 31-16 in the conference semifinals. Meanwhile, Dallas went on to top the Rams 34-13 in the wild-card game. They followed that by winning a squeaker against the Falcons 30-27 in the other conference semifinal. That set up the NFL championship game.

"The week before the game, coach Dick Vermeil took the entire squad to Tampa to practice to take them away from all the hoopla and distractions back in Philly. Vermeil's move in doing that was—well, put it this way, this was Vermeil at the top of his game. The whole week before the game when he and the team were in Tampa, he downplayed the Eagles' chances. He lamented that the Eagles were not only battered and bruised, but outmanned at virtually every position. I had a personal thrill that week, too. I did a simulcast on both Philly's WIP and Dallas' KRLD. It was called the 'Tale of Two Cities' with Brad Sham, a guy who had been the Cowboys play-by-play man for years.

"In any event, the stage was set for the big game, the one Vermeil had been aiming for since he took the team over. This was the long-awaited showdown against Dallas in the NFC championship game. The Eagles were ready, and so was every Philadelphia fan."

THE GAME OF MY LIFE
JANUARY 11, 1981

Merrill Reese: "It was a horrible day, bitter cold. The Vet was packed—70,696 screaming fans. The feeling in that stadium was electric. Vermeil had the team so well prepared, and the fans were so ready. As cold a day as it was, I don't think anyone in the stands noticed it at all.

"Of course, as far as memories of the game itself go, everyone remembers the Wilbert Montgomery 42-yard TD run. But I remember other plays that set the tone. John Bunting simply buried Tony Dorsett early in the game. He stopped Dorsett for no gain, and I think the hit sent Dallas a message. Dorsett was one of the most electric runners I ever saw—a threat to go coast to coast every time he touched the ball. After the Bunting hit, I started to believe. I could almost see the intensity of this team. If any coach ever had a team at its peak for a game, it was Vermeil for this one.

"I'll admit I had my doubts. Before the game, I thought, 'This is Dallas, and I've had my heart broken so many times before!' I really didn't want to allow myself to get my hopes too high. I fully expected the game would go right down to the wire, but that's not how it played out. Sure, the game was tied 7-7 at halftime. But then Tony Franklin hit a 26-yard field goal early in the second half, and from then on, the Eagles never looked back. Leroy Harris smashed over on a 1-yard run a little while later and stretched the lead to 10 points in the fourth quarter.

"But, yes, when I think of that game, the enduring image will always be the Montgomery TD run in the first quarter. Wilbert took the handoff from Jaworski and ran behind two big blocks by Jerry Sizemore and Woody Peoples. It was a beautiful sight, Wilbert breaking into the open field through that huge hole. Once Wilbert saw daylight, there was no one catching him. When I saw that play, I thought the same thing that everyone in the Delaware Valley thought: I just knew the Eagles were going to the Super Bowl.

"And that's why I'd choose this game as the game of my life. That one play, Wilbert's big run in the big game against Dallas, gave me a feeling I've never had before or since. I knew the Eagles were Super Bowl bound."

Chapter 18

BILL BERGEY

"SO, WHAT WAS THE GAME OF YOUR LIFE?"

Bill Bergey: "I've got to say the game I remember most was the NFC championship game against Dallas—the game we won 20-7. I didn't play my best game that day, but it was the greatest game I can think of. After my knee surgery the year before, I never really got back to 100 percent. I think I might have been playing at about 65 percent effectiveness that year. But that game sticks out so much because it was the game that we achieved the success we had worked so hard for all during the Vermeil years."

Bill came to the Eagles in 1974 via a trade with the Bengals which stipulated that Philly give up a first-round draft pick in 1977 as well as first- and second-round picks in 1978. No Philadelphian ever rued the trade. Standing 6-foot-2 and weighing 243 pounds, Bill racked up close to 1,200 bone-jarring tackles (233 of which came in a single season) and picked off 18 passes in seven seasons. He set and held the club record for most interceptions by a linebacker. He was honored as All-Pro five consecutive seasons. He was a four-time Pro Bowler and three-time Eagles MVP. His spirited play and the role he embraced as team leader earned him election to the Eagles Honor Roll in 1988.

HOW WELL DO YOU KNOW YOUR BIRDS?

Which Eagle made the most consecutive Pro Bowl appearances?

a) Tommy McDonald
b) Pete Retzlaff
c) Chuck Bednarik
d) Donovan McNabb
e) Reggie White
f) Eric Allen
g) Mike Quick
h) Norm "Wild Man" Willey

MEET BILL BERGEY

William Earl Bergey was born on February 9, 1945, and was raised in South Dayton, New York. He played football at South Dayton High School before leaving for college at Arkansas State, where he earned All-America honors. He has been honored as the Top Player in Arkansas State University history, and his name still speckles the Indians' record book. He set the school standard for most fumble recoveries in a season, most tackles in a game, most tackles in a season, and most career tackles—not a bad career. His 1968 average of 19.6 tackles per game is off the charts. He played in three postseason all-star games during his ASU career and was selected to the All-Southland Conference team three times and to the Southland Conference All-First Decade team. Bergey's jersey number, 66—a familiar sight at Veterans Stadium a few years later—was retired by ASU in 1997.

When Bill graduated from college, the American Football League was still a separate entity from the National Football League. Each league vied for the same talent. In 1969, Bill was a second-round choice of the AFL Cincinnati Bengals. He immediately earned a starting berth and was selected to the AFL All-Star team as a rookie. After five standout seasons with Cincinnati, he came to the Eagles in a trade. Bill immediately stepped up as team leader. His drive and grit helped build the team into a Super Bowl squad.

Bill Bergey (No. 66) speaks with an opponent as the Eagles celebrate a victory. *AP Images*

BUILDING UP TO THE GAME

"Before the 1980 season," Bill Bergey relates, "Vermeil said to me, 'Bill, help me get Dallas.' So I did. I dedicated myself to beating Dallas that year, all year. I was near the end of my career and I knew it. I wasn't going to have another shot at playing in a Super Bowl, so that's what I set out to do. It's what all of us set out to do.

"Of course, Dick had been focused on catching Dallas from day one, as soon as he arrived from UCLA. He told us Dallas was the standard for excellence and we were going to work our butts off and overtake them. I think the first game he ever coached was against Dallas. [It was, and Dallas whopped the Birds 27-7.] I think that first game he saw that we were outclassed, and that became his focus: setting up a program for catching and overtaking Dallas.

"He came into Philly with all his tough notions and philosophies about practicing hard and working hard. It was a different approach than I had ever seen. I said to myself that I was going with his program all the way. But his program did work for us. He got the kind of ballplayers he wanted and stuck by them. By the time we got to 1980, there were maybe five guys left from the roster the day he walked in. Three of those guys were in the linebacking corps: John Bunting, Frank LeMaster, and me.

"Anyway, getting back to 1980, we split our regular-season games with Dallas. We played them down there in the last game of the regular season and they gave us a scare. To win the division, we had to beat them by 25 points. They got ahead of us by 27 at one point in the game, but we came back and narrowed the lead. We lost the game, but came out of the game with the division title in hand.

"When we got to play Dallas in the NFC championship game, Dick Vermeil was at his ultimate. He flew the team down to Tampa Bay the week before the game because it was so cold in Philly that week. He wanted us to get a week of focused practices in, and we did. We had the best practice week I've ever seen. Vermeil pushed every possible hot button we had that week. He challenged us, fired us up. He was really pushing Jerry Sizemore. That week, Jerry was calling Vermeil's challenges 'harsh,' but they turned out to be just what Jerry needed. He seemed to find the right button for each guy.

"I'll tell you this, going into that game, our feeling was not were we going to beat Dallas, but how bad were we going to beat them. I never experienced a feeling that strong in my life. Coming down that runway before the game, we felt unstoppable. When we ran out of the runway, my wife, who was in the stands, said to my two boys, Jason and Jake, 'Your dad's going to the Super Bowl!' She said she could feel the confidence up in the stands."

THE GAME OF MY LIFE
JANUARY 11, 1981

Bill Bergey: "On game day, Vermeil was still looking for every possible edge. He had noticed—we all noticed—that Dallas never seemed to win when they wore their pukey blue jerseys. So we chose to wear white and forced them to wear their pukey blue jerseys. I think after they lost that day, they ditched those ugly things for good!

"I never felt such cohesiveness in the defensive unit. I looked down the defensive line that day with guys like Charley Johnson and Claude Humphrey and the rest. I could feel that everyone out there was playing every second of that game to win. I think if you checked the statistics for the five years prior to that season, we had about the best defense in football. We had developed so much confidence from playing successfully together. We stopped Dallas dead. The score was 20-7, but that doesn't tell the story. We beat the living hell out of them.

"So many guys were such great performers for us that year. Ron Jaworski was the NFC Player of the Year. I think Wilbert Montgomery gained close to 200 yards that day, didn't he? [Wilbert gained 194 yards: two yards short of Steve Van Buren's Eagles playoff rushing record of 196 yards in the 1949 NFL championship game versus the L.A. Rams.] What a game! Even guys like Petey Perot, who was not a super talent but gave 100 percent all the time—I remember him on Randy White, that big Dallas tackle from Maryland. After the whistle blew, there would be Petey, holding his block and keeping on, which really got Randy upset. After the game, White was complaining about the Eagles being a bunch of hairy high schoolers because we were so emotional.

"When we got back in the locker room after the game, Leonard Tose had Dom Perignon champagne in there waiting for us. He grabbed us all while we were whooping and hollering and warned us, 'This champagne is for drinking, not squirting at each other!' My kids were in the locker room with me. It was such a celebration, and it didn't end there!

"After the game, I took a bunch of my old friends from Buffalo to dinner. They had come down for the game. My wife and I and all of my Buffalo friends were in my van headed to the city for dinner at the Saloon in South Philly. We had a weird thing happen en route. There was a girl on the passenger's side in the car in front of us. Every red light or stop sign, she'd get out and take another article of clothing off! I'm not kidding! [Hey Bill, what happens in Philly stays in Philly.] I pointed it out to everyone in the van and said, 'The heck with dinner! Let's follow this van and see what happens!' My wife had a different idea. So we ditched that idea and went to dinner. We had more Dom Perignon. One of our friends from Buffalo, Joan, ordered a 22-ounce steak. Somehow, it landed on the floor with the knife in it, and Joan just kept drinking more champagne! It was one of those nights—just an amazing celebration!

"The next day, though, I couldn't walk. My knee was so swollen. Whatever I had, I left on that field. When Dr. Vince DiStefano drained my knee the next day, he said he never saw anything like it. You know how they draw back on that syringe to fill the tube? He didn't have to. The fluid pressure in my knee pushed it back all by itself. The tube filled up in seconds.

"So yeah, that's still my greatest memory. It wasn't my best game by a long shot, but the excitement, the feeling of accomplishment—that was tops."

WRAP

"I think we were so high for that game that it was like our Super Bowl," Bill Bergey explains. "We had been after Dallas for so long. Of course, we had one game left, the Super Bowl, and we didn't fare too well in it. That wasn't Dick Vermeil's fault. He kept it up—kept driving, kept thinking, kept working, kept being Dick Vermeil. Before the Super Bowl, he arranged for Woody Hayes and Don Rickles to come in and speak to the team. We just fell short. We were flat and didn't play a good game."

As for his knee, Bergey explains, "I got a knee replacement a few years back. The Eagles were great about it. I went down at the Novacare Center to rehab, and I couldn't be more pleased with the treatment and the way my knee turned out. I have great mobility. Nowadays, I walk about five to nine miles a day and keep it in shape."

Bill, who resides in Chadds Ford, Pennsylvania, is also busy as a partner in a concern that invests in real estate countrywide, but particularly on the east coast. "From about August 1 until the Super Bowl, I'm real busy with the business as well as with the Eagles. I do the pre- and postgame radio for them and make lots of personal appearances and the like. Then I slow it down for the next five, six months. I've got five grandchildren at this point, and I make sure I spend as much of my time with them as possible."

"HOW WELL DO YOU KNOW YOUR BIRDS?" ANSWER
e) Reggie White (He made seven consecutive All-Pro appearances.)

Chapter 19

GREG BROWN

"SO, WHAT WAS THE GAME OF YOUR LIFE?"

Greg Brown: "I guess the biggest highlight of my career was just getting the chance to play professional football! I wasn't drafted, but my college coach got me a chance to talk to Dick Vermeil and to earn a spot. After that, all the games were all a thrill, but since I grew up in Washington D.C., I guess my biggest thrills were always when we played against the Redskins. And I'll pick my very first game against the 'Skins as a rookie as the game of my life."

Greg Brown got his big break when Dick Vermeil gave him a shot at making the Eagles squad. And make it he did. Greg fit right into the aggressive three defensive linemen set that helped the Eagles reach the Super Bowl in 1980. The 6-foot-5 competitor was a vital acquisition and saw a lot of action as a backup in his 1981 rookie season. The Eagles unfortunately suffered a precipitous decline starting in 1982, Dick Vermeil's last year as head coach. Marion Campbell, the Swamp Fox of the 1960 Eagles, filled Vermeil's vacancy. Greg became a starter during Campbell's tenure and manned the trenches till the arrival of Buddy Ryan. Greg left for Atlanta at that point. He toiled as a Falcon for a couple of seasons before calling it quits. Eagles fans will always remember Greg as a good pass rusher and a hard-nosed interior lineman.

HOW WELL DO YOU KNOW YOUR BIRDS?

Only two Eagles running backs have ever rushed for more than 200 yards in a regular-season game. Pick the two from the list below.

a) Wilbert Montgomery
b) Steve Van Buren
c) Bosh Pritchard
d) Tim Brown
e) Duce Staley
f) Billy Ray Barnes
g) Swede Hanson
h) Brian Westbrook
i) Ricky Watters
j) Tom Woodeshick
k) Clarence Peaks
l) Charley Garner

MEET GREG BROWN

When Gregory Lee Brown bade Kansas State adieu in 1980, he left undrafted and uncertain about the career he yearned for in professional football. "Fortunately, Coach Vermeil gave me a shot." Greg had played three years at Kansas State University before transferring to Eastern Illinois. By NCAA rules, his transfer necessitated sitting out a year. Greg got restless and left school. He returned to Washington, D.C., and earned his pay in construction for two years. His ex-line coach at Eastern Illinois visited him and induced the Eagles to take a look at Greg. "I went to the mini-camp and met with the defensive line coach, Chuck Clausen, who thought I was too small at first. They were looking at lots of guys. I don't know how many, exactly. I did the agility drills and then ran about a 4.2 40, the same as Wilbert Montgomery's. They invited me back to training camp and told me to put on 15 to 20 pounds."

Greg reported to camp at about 220 pounds. After following a strict regimen of caloric eating, he upped his heft to 265 pounds by the start of the season. The beefier Greg Brown made an auspicious NFL debut, registering two sacks in a 24-10 opening-game victory over the Giants.

Greg reflects, "I had a good career in football. I had great days and some great memories." As a backup his rookie season, Greg helped the Eagles rush out-sack opponents by a factor of almost two to one: 40 to 22. In the nine-game strike-shortened season of 1982, again as a spot player, Greg tallied 4.5 sacks, second only to team leader Dennis Harrison's 10.5. With Greg still fulfilling a backup role the following season, the Harrison-Brown duo again ranked one-two in Eagles sacks. (Harrison had 11, Brown had 8.5.)

Greg took over the duties at right defensive end upon the departure of Carl Hairston in 1984. This time he led the team in sacks, bettering second-place Dennis Harrison 16.0 to 12.0. Greg also ranked second on the team in tackles behind leader Jerry Robinson. In 1985, Greg achieved parity in sacks with future Hall of Famer Reggie White. Each sacked 13.0 would-be passers. What's more, Greg registered 124 tackles (second best on the team) to the Minister of Defense's 100.

With the dawn of the Buddy Ryan era, Greg survived Ryan's 20-player purge of the 1985 roster. Greg's nine sacks placed a distant second to Reggie White's team-leading 18.0. Greg also recorded 88 tackles, which ranked fifth among Eagles defenders.

In 1987, No. 89 was dealt to Atlanta in exchange for DE/DT Mike Pitts. Greg closed out his career after two Falcons campaigns.

Greg lives in southern Jersey. He remains a big Eagles fan and is enjoying retirement as a granddad.

BUILDING UP TO THE GAME

After losing the Super Bowl in 1980, the Eagles roared out of the gate in '81. They beat the Giants, New England, and Buffalo in succession. Next up was division-rival Washington, who came into the Vet looking to topple the high-flying Birds.

Philadelphia was hungrier than ever for their Iggles to go all the way. Since the Birds fell tantalizingly short of copping the Lombardi Trophy the previous season, most fans thought 1981 was to be the long-awaited year. The roster had changed little. In the coaching ranks, the Eagles added Harry Gamble, former Penn coach. Three rookies nudged their way on the roster itself: CB Ray Ellis, DE Leonard Mitchell, and DE Greg Brown.

Greg Brown was particularly pumped up for the upcoming 'Skins game as a Washington, D.C., native and a lifetime Washington fan. Born in D.C. on January 5, 1957, the big lineman played his high school football at Howard D. Woodson High. Greg's family contingent was in the stands that day. Naturally, they were rabidly rooting for … Washington! "Yeah, I have nine sisters and brothers. They were all there with my mom and they're all lifelong Redskin fans. It's not that they didn't want me to do well in the game. They just wanted Washington to win!"

THE GAME OF MY LIFE
SEPTEMBER 27, 1981

Greg Brown: "I scored my one and only NFL touchdown that day. It was a thrill since I was only a rookie and it came against Washington. The Redskins weren't doing too well at that point [they were 0-3], but they're always dangerous because of the divisional rivalry between them and the Eagles. I was facing off with Joe Jacobi, one of the best offensive linemen in the business, and I had a good day. That was rewarding.

"As for the game itself, our whole team got off to a bad start that day. Our offense scored first—I think Jaws threw a TD. [Jaworski hit Louie Giammona on a 13-yard strike.] But that was our only score in the first half. Fortunately, we got down to playing Eagles football in the second half. We shut them down pretty good after the first half.

"In the second half, our D really started hitting them. Ken Clarke threw Joe Theisman for a safety [the Eagles' first safety since 1972]. We had a real big fourth quarter when we put the game way out of reach. [The Birds scored 22 points in the final stanza.] That's when I scored my touchdown! I recovered a fumble [Washington backup QB Tom Flick coughed the pigskin up] and I scooped it up and ran it in 7 yards for a score.

"That's a pretty great game to look back on. My family was there and saw my only touchdown. I was a rookie playing on a great squad that had played in the Super Bowl the year before. Our defensive line was real tight my whole time. It was like a boys club. Once you were in it, you were accepted forever. We got to know each other's moves and we could anticipate what each of the other guys on the line would do in any given situation. I felt like I fit in fast and got to execute pretty well with the guys that had been working together for a number of years."

WRAP

The Eagles' victory that day tied them with Dallas at 4-0 for the top spot in the division. Louie Giammona filled in for the injured Wilbert Montgomery and responded with a big day. It was vindication for

Giammona in a couple of ways. The 5-foot-9, 180-pound running back from Utah State had been drafted by the Jets in 1976, even though he was overlooked because of his size. He saw limited duty as a Jets rookie, missed his entire sophomore year with a blown-out knee, and was cut in the Jets' '78 training camp. The Eagles signed him shortly thereafter, at which point Louie shouldered another albatross. Louie was Coach Vermeil's nephew. Thus, his performance this day was personally gratifying. Louie had a productive though not spectacular day, rushing 18 times for 49 yards and hauling in five passes for 47 yards, including a 13-yard scoring pass.

In the second half, as Greg Brown points out, the Birds hit on all cylinders. Giammona scored on a 1-yard plunge. Jaworski hit Charlie Smith on a 29-yard TD. (Washington QB Joe Theismann put up decent numbers in the contest, completing 22 of 32 for 265 yards, while his Eagles counterpart, Jaworski, turned in a more plebian 14-for-26 and 150 yards.) Tony Franklin nailed two field goals of 28 and 36 yards. The Birds' defense, which had yielded a whopping 265 first-half yards, tightened up and limited the 'Skins to 72 yards. In the lopsided fourth-period action, the Birds' defense forced three turnovers and registered a safety.

"HOW WELL DO YOU KNOW YOUR BIRDS?" ANSWER
b) Steve Van Buren (204 yards vs. the Pittsburgh Steelers on 11/27/49) and **e)** Duce Staley (201 yards vs. the Dallas Cowboys on 9/4/00)

Chapter 20

GARRY COBB

"SO, WHAT WAS THE GAME OF YOUR LIFE?"

G-Cobb: "I had some big games with Detroit and Dallas, too, but Philly was the greatest time of my career. And if you want the most memorable game in my mind that I played in Philly, that's easy. It was in 1986: the Philadelphia Eagles versus the Atlanta Falcons in Atlanta. I had my best day ever."

Philadelphia knows him as G-Cobb. His longtime trademark expression around Philly is "G-Cobb in the House." Garry has been in the Philly house for a number of years. He was drafted by Dallas in the ninth round of the 1979 draft. The Cowboys cut him, but the Lions picked him up on waivers. He starred in Motown for half a decade before being dealt to Philadelphia in 1985 for Eagles legend Wilbert Montgomery. Cobb ended his NFL career in 1989 as a Dallas Cowboy. He picked off 10 interceptions and recorded 23.5 sacks in a distinguished 10-year NFL career. Since 1997, G-Cobb has been a sports reporter for Philadelphia's Channel 3 Eyewitness News team as well as a host on Philly's WIP Radio.

HOW WELL DO YOU KNOW YOUR BIRDS?

The Eagles have had only two players chosen as NFL Rookie of the Year. One won the award in 1951, the other in 1988. They both played the same position. What position did they play?

a) Linebacker
c) Tight end
e) Defensive back
g) Running back

b) Quarterback
d) Wide receiver
f) Kicker
h) Center

MEET G-COBB

Garry Cobb was born in Carthage, Georgia, on March 16, 1957. His family later moved north, settling in New England. Garry attended high school in Stamford, Connecticut, where he starred not only in basketball and baseball, but also in football. Garry was heavily recruited. He chose to migrate cross-country to play college football. He attended USC in Los Angeles. The ex-linebacker confesses that he made his college choice while watching the most painful game in the history of Notre Dame football—for Irish fans, that is. USC humiliated Notre Dame 55-24 that day. The lopsided score doesn't reflect the true horror of the Irish setback. USC was on the bottom end of a 24-6 score at halftime. The curtain almost dropped on the first half with the Irish ahead 24-0. However, at the close of the half, Trojan RB Anthony Davis ran a kickoff coast to coast for a TD.

The second half was dreadful. In the last two quarters alone, the Trojans laid a 49-0 shellacking on the shell-shocked South Benders. It was this USC comeback that G-Cobb and the rest of the nation watched bug-eyed that convinced the Connecticut high school senior to traipse cross country. Garry decided he simply had to be part of the USC program as he watched the slaughter incredulously from his couch. After that game, USC defensive back coach Wayne Fontes had little trouble recruiting Garry.

Linebacker Garry Cobb waits for play to resume against the San Francisco 49ers on November 3, 1985. *George Rose/Getty Images*

Garry never regretted his decision. He admits to beguilement at the glitz and glitter of Hollywood. California's nonstop sunshine enchanted him, too. When the young recruit trotted on to the field at his first USC training camp, however, the intensity level he encountered took him aback. John McKay was the USC coach—the same John McKay with four national championships already bulleted on his CV. McKay's philosophy centered upon working his charges to the bone at practice all week. McKay believed this approach   made the games themselves a cakewalk.

G-Cobb gives much credit for his own aggressive style of play to a little fireplug named Marty Goux, a USC defensive coach. Garry recalls passing the "Goux Guts Test" as his personal USC initiation. Normally in intra-squad scrimmages, each combatant remained on the field for three or four plays before surrendering his spot to somebody on the next unit. On this particular day, each time the units changed, Garry was ordered to remain on the field. Each time he started to head for the sidelines for a breather, he was told to stay put. Garry languished on the field for one grueling series after another. He spent the better part of the afternoon getting bowled over by huge tight ends and linemen perfecting USC's feared "Student Body" (left or right) sweeps.

But the Connecticut kid hung tough. His seemingly interminable and unanticipated "sentence" to unmitigated action finally ended on the next-to-last play of the scrimmage. Garry emerged from a pile of huge bodies and felt a hearty slap on his pads. It was Coach Goux, who extended a hand to him and told him he had passed the "Guts Test."

Goux used to slap a player's helmet expressly to make his own hand bleed. Then he'd lick the blood and declare, "This is USC football. Blood and guts!" The glee of the zealot eager to sacrifice himself for the purpose of destroying any enemy was the sagacious gift he imparted to his players.

As Garry found out during his Trojan days, Goux happened to harbor a "special" disdain for Notre Dame. The giver of the "Guts Test" played for USC in the '50s. His favorite games were the USC-Notre Dame battles, which he termed "big man on big man" football—an ironic characterization given Goux's 5-foot-6 frame. As it turns out, Goux was injured in one of those Trojan-Irish battles and apparently didn't hear the final gun sound at the end of the contest. He played Ahab to Notre Dame's Moby Dick. Head coach John McKay used to abdicate the pregame pep talk to Coach Goux when Notre Dame was the opponent. Garry calls Goux's tirades the fieriest pregame talks he's ever heard.

Garry enjoyed a stellar career at USC's football factory. Holding down a linebacker slot for the Trojans, he started on teams that won two Rose Bowls and one national championship. Of course, though Garry was a big fish, he was also in a very big pond. His teammates read like a who's who of collegiate football. Two of his college mates, Charles White and Marcus Allen, won Heisman Trophies. Three fellow players—Marcus Allen, Ronnie Lott, and Anthony Munoz—became Pro Football Hall of Famers. Gary Jeter, Marvin Powell, Ricky Bell, Clay Matthews, Rod Martin, David Lewis, Larry McGrew, Larry Braziel, Brad Budde, Roy Foster, Keith Van Horne, Dennis Thurman, Eric Williams, Dennis Smith, Rich Dimmler, Donnie Hickman, Chris Foote, Lynn Cain, William Gay, Hobe Brenner, Dennis Johnson, Jeff Fisher, Carter Hartwig, Riki Ellison, and Calvin Sweeney all inked pro contracts. Aswim in that huge talent pool, G-Cobb nonetheless managed to distinguish himself with his selection to the 1978 All-PAC team.

Both the California Angels and Chicago Cubs offered Garry a baseball contract. A ninth-round Dallas Cowboy pick, G-Cobb opted for professional football instead. The depth of the USC talent pool had wowed Garry, but he would be downright gobsmacked at the Cowboys' training camp.

When Garry came to camp, he Cowboys were coming off a Super Bowl tussle against Pittsburgh in the heyday of the Steelers' "Steel Curtain." Big stars like Roger Staubach, Tony Dorsett, Drew Pearson, Randy White, Harvey Martin, Mike Ditka, and Cliff Harris studded the roster. Dallas' star power rivaled that of Tinseltown. In fact, Big D boasted its own piece of self-proclaimed Hollywood in linebacker Thomas Henderson. Henderson dubbed himself "Hollywood" Henderson. The name stuck for each remaining minute of his 15 minutes of fame.

The 'Boys made a rare mistake in G-Cobb's case. They cut him. But the Detroit Lions picked up Garry on waivers. Garry toiled on Detroit special teams for a couple of years, but battled his way to a starting berth in his third year there. He responded with three 100-plus tackle seasons and was chosen team captain for two years. Contract disputes led to a trade. Garry came to Philadelphia in exchange for Wilbert Montgomery.

As an Eagle, No. 50 started for three years—no mean feat given the caliber of the Eagles defense in that era. Seth Joyner, Reggie White, Jerome Brown, Eric Allen, Andre Waters, Wes Hopkins, and a host of others teamed to make the Birds defense the cream of the NFL crop. When G-Cobb left Philly in 1988, his career went full circle. He closed out his career as a leading light for the then-rebuilding Cowboys, topping the team in sacks with 7.5. He retired in 1989.

After his football career, Garry worked for Philly's WIP Radio and Philly's Channel 3, where he shares insights along with fellow ex-pro footballer Beasley Reece. G-Cobb and his family settled in Cherry Hill, a bustling enclave across the Delaware River from the Quaker City. His son, Garry, excelled athletically at Cherry Hill East High, where he earned All-South Jersey honors his junior and senior year. Like his dad, the younger Cobb was heavily recruited, and like his dad, he opted for a West Coast school. Garry starred on the gridiron at Stanford before going to Rutgers for a law degree.

BUILDING UP TO THE GAME

The '86 Eagles were off to a rocky start under brand new head coach Buddy Ryan. The irascible Ryan had already chiseled a reputation as a headstrong, sometimes recklessly opinionated character when he was the defensive coordinator under the mighty Mike Ditka-led Bears of the early and mid-'80s. Ryan was encountering increased difficulty finding his requisite light under the shadow of his head coach, the media-conscious Ditka. When Eagles owner Norman Braman offered Ryan his first head coaching job, Buddy eagerly accepted and savored the new top-dog role.

Buddy inherited a 7-9 team. From the get-go, he strived to obliterate every vestige of it, or so many contemporary observers insisted. He summarily dumped 20 players from the prior year. The departed included fan-favorite Herman Edwards, who, over the course of 135 consecutive Eagles games, nabbed 33 enemy passes. That figure fell one short of Bill Bradley's club record. New faces like RB Keith Byars, the Birds' No. 1 draft choice, DE Clyde Simmons, and FS Terry Hoag dominated the roster in the first year of Buddy ball.

In '86, the Eagles emerged slowly at 1-3, but managed a win over the Rams that showed defensive muscle. They headed to Atlanta believing they may have started to jell.

THE GAME OF MY LIFE
OCTOBER 5, 1986

G-Cobb: "We were hot that day. The defense was really smoking! Once we stopped the Atlanta running game, they had to pass. Buddy loved that situation. He just kept sending us and we kept putting the pressure on the quarterback. The defense loved that kind of game. Poor David Archer, the Atlanta quarterback! The guy couldn't win for losing. All he saw was green. See, we had Reggie White and Ken Clarke and Byron Darby up front, and those guys always seemed to manage to get in on the QB. Buddy had Reggie lining up in the middle to keep the pressure coming from the middle. I was coming from the outside, and it seems like just about every time I happened to get to Archer faster—just a step faster—than Reggie. I'll tell you, Reggie was always in there. He was relentless! I had four sacks that day, and I think every time I got up from the pile, Reggie was standing over me, a step away from getting the sack himself. The big advantage that Reggie being in the middle gave me was that it prevented David Archer from stepping up into the pocket to avoid the outside rush. I know Archer was getting frustrated by having nowhere to turn. You know, those four sacks I had, they were real shots. I really jolted the quarterback. He never saw the hits coming. He'd get up from the pile and kind of look around bewildered, like, 'Where'd he come from?'

"I remember we got the lead fairly early. Mike Quick made an awesome one-handed grab in the end zone to put us in front. But you know, our offense hadn't really clicked yet. Not only that, Atlanta had a strong defense, too. They ranked fourth in team defense that year. They weren't pushovers. But I don't think Atlanta moved the ball past midfield more than one time that game. We caused so many turnovers and stayed in good field position all day long. The offense just had trouble capitalizing.

"But that doesn't take anything away from the D. What a great effort! I was fortunate that day. On a couple of those sacks, I beat their running back a few times. I think it was William Andrews. And the Falcons just never really figured out how to stop us. But really, I don't think we could have been stopped that day. We turned in a shutout. It was a day when the defense got to experience firsthand how much fun it is to play Buddy's 46 defense. Aggressive guys like the ones on that defense love that alignment. It frees you up to take chances and really make things happen."

WRAP

In one memorable game, G-Cobb recorded two-thirds of his sacks for the entire '86 season. In another memorable game, he recorded close to 20 percent of his career sacks. His exploits earned him Defensive Player of the Week honors and made him a perennial favorite of Vet Stadium's 700-level.

"HOW WELL DO YOU KNOW YOUR BIRDS?" ANSWER
c) Tight end (Bobby Walston won in 1951, Keith Jackson in 1988. There is a little zooker to this question. The tight end position was not listed as a separate position till 1966 in *Pro Football Encyclopedia*. However, Walston did play the "closed end" position with the Eagles his entire career, even on the 1960 championship team. Pete Retzlaff did not assume the tight end slot till Walston retired. Retzlaff was a split end on the '60 offense.)

Chapter 21

MIKE QUICK

"SO, WHAT WAS THE GAME OF YOUR LIFE?"

Mike Quick: "I'll bet my answer will surprise a lot of fans. I think a lot of Eagles fans think they could answer that question for me. They'd say it was the game against Atlanta when I caught the 99-yard touchdown pass—the longest pass completion ever. But actually, the game that first comes to my mind is the game against the Raiders. That's because of the level of competition I faced that day. I caught three touchdown passes from Randall going against one of the best defensive backfields ever. I think that game gave me as much personal satisfaction as I ever got."

Mike Quick ranks second behind Pete Retzlaff in TD passes caught by an Eagles receiver. The five-time Pro Bowler's name is ubiquitous in the Eagles' all-time record book. The soft-spoken wide receiver with deceptive speed was a Philly favorite who spent his entire nine-year career making great catches in the City of Brotherly Love. For the past nine years, he has teamed with Merrill Reese as the color man on the Eagles Radio Network.

HOW WELL DO YOU KNOW YOUR BIRDS?

On the Eagles all-time roster, only two players' last names begin with "Q." One, of course, is Mike Quick (duh). Who is the other?

(He is mentioned elsewhere in this book. Hint: He wore jersey No. 83, but not when he intercepted the Eagles' first pass in the 1960 championship game.)

MEET MIKE QUICK

Michael Anthony Quick, born May 14, 1959, in North Carolina, starred with the NC State Wolfpack in college. He was the Eagles' No. 1 draft choice in 1982. He rewarded that vote of confidence with a stellar, record-setting career spent entirely in green and white. Mike's 1,409 yards in 1983 rank No. 1 on the Eagles' all-time list in receiving yards for a single season, while his 13 TDs in 1983 place him at No. 2 for most receiving touchdowns in a season. The 6-foot-2, 190-pound athlete is tied with Hall of Famer Pete Pihos for the Eagles' top spot in number of consecutive games catching a TD pass. His six 100-yard receiving games in a single season place him at No. 2 on the Birds' all-time list for most games in a single season with 100 or more receiving yards. Only one Eagles receiver has strung together more consecutive games with 100 or more yards receiving than Mike's four. His 1985 season was particularly sensational as No. 82 topped the NFL in yards gained on pass receptions (1,247) and TD passes caught (11). He also caught the NFL's longest-ever TD pass that same year.

The sight of Mike Quick wresting the ball away in a crowd of defenders or breaking clear on bump-and-run coverage was a familiar one to the Vet Stadium crowd. His long, loping stride gave him the deceptive speed that made him a feared, respected, deep threat.

BUILDING UP TO THE GAME

The Eagles were in a retooling mode in 1986, Buddy Ryan's first season at the helm. After Mike Quick's 1985 campaign, in which he led the NFL both in receiving yards and TDs caught, he cooled down slightly in 1986—but not enough to prevent his fourth consecutive selection to the All-Pro squad.

On November 30, 1986, wide receiver Mike Quick scores one of three touchdowns against the Los Angeles Raiders. The Eagles won 33-27 in overtime. *George Rose/Getty Images*

Despite an abysmal 3-9 record, the Eagles squad was starting to flash some of the feistiness and pride that would soon become its hallmark. Although the Birds were out of the running for the playoffs, they brought their grit to L.A. to face the Raiders late in the season. L.A. was in the thick of the scrape for the playoffs and looking for a relatively easy victory.

"Personally, I had a lot of pride going into that game," Mike Quick recalls. "I knew I was going against two of the best defensive backfield guys in the business, Mike Haines and Lester Hayes. In addition to the challenge of the game itself, I was looking forward to a big personal challenge."

THE GAME OF MY LIFE
NOVEMBER 30, 1986

Mike Quick: "This was Buddy Ryan's first season. I think we were starting to jell under Buddy's system, even though the results weren't there yet. We weren't going anywhere that season, but we weren't lying down for anyone, either. We took the field every week scrapping for a win, regardless of our playoff status.

"I was particularly up for this game because I wanted those two guys, Lester Hayes and Mike Haynes, to come out respecting me as one of the game's best receivers. They respected me going into the game, and actually, I was a bit surprised. Those guys had earned such a reputation for playing tough and physical that I expected the game to be a bit more physical than it was. They threw a lot of man-to-man coverage on me, more than I expected. Lester had me one-on-one, and I thought he was going to get more help.

"I don't know if you remember Lester and his thing with the stick 'um. Back then, lots of receivers and defensive backs put that sticky stuff all over their hands. I think Lester smeared it all over his whole uniform! Anyway, I watched film all week of these guys. They manhandled a lot of receivers and talked a lot during the game, so that's the kind of treatment I was expecting. But they were surprisingly quiet, too. Not that it mattered—talking trash wouldn't have thrown me off my game. I was focused. So was the whole team.

"Over the years, I've gotten to know those guys pretty well from golf tournaments and other events. I still joke with them about that day!

"I ended up catching three touchdown passes. Lots of guys on our team had big games [including Andre Waters, who also picked this game as the game of his life]. Like I said, you could feel us starting to jell as a team and starting to play Eagles football. We took a lot from that win—taking the Raiders to overtime in a must-win game for them. They were in a dogfight with Denver for the title and they needed a W. It was a big character builder and boost for us to take the game from them in overtime in their own yard in front of their famous crowd [that would be the Raider Nation—which has now been relegated to a distant second place in 'nation' status behind the Colbert Nation].

"I always tell my current sidekick in the radio booth, Merrill Reese, that he made the call of my life, since we're talking about the game of my life. I have a tape of that Raiders game. On one of my TDs, Merrill said, 'A quarterback finding Mike Quick is like a prospector finding gold!' I liked that one!

"As for the game itself, we came in as heavy underdogs. We had lost four in a row. … I caught three TDs and Gregg Garrity ran a punt back for another touchdown. Then, in the sudden-death period, the Raiders had the ball and were moving on us. It looked like we were done. The Raiders were at our 16-yard line. They tried to play it safe, and their QB [Jim Plunkett] handed the ball to Marcus Allen, who took it up the middle so they'd be in good field goal position. But Seth Joyner stripped the ball, and Andre [Waters] scooped it up and ran it downfield. They didn't catch up to Andre till he was down at their 4-yard line. A couple plays later, Randall [Cunningham] sneaked over for the win.

"I think that win might have opened the door to the success we started to achieve in the next few seasons."

WRAP

In addition to his three TD catches, Mike finished the Raiders game with eight receptions for 145 yards. Philadelphia prevailed despite allowing an all-time club high for sacks (11). The Eagles lost two of their remaining three games after that victory over the Raiders. However, a few stars of the Buddy Ryan-era Eagles were starting to ascend. So were a few of the fundamental flaws that would clip the Eagles' wings as a Super Bowl team. Despite a 5-10 season that year, Reggie White broke the club record for sacks with 18, while Keith Byars broke Billy Ray Barnes' 1957 club record for rushing yards by a rookie. Unfortunately, as Buddy Ryan would bemoan in later years, the weak offensive line, as well as the imbalance in the prowess of the offensive and defensive units started to gestate. Eagles punter John Teltschick's record number of punts (108) was a dubious feat that smashed Spike Jones' standard (94) set on the hapless 1976 squad. The propensity for drawing penalties flared up, too. The team's 901 penalty yards shattered the previous standard of 855 assessed in 1981.

"HOW WELL DO YOU KNOW YOUR BIRDS?" ANSWER
Bill Quinlan

Chapter 22

ANDRE WATERS

"SO, WHAT WAS THE GAME OF YOUR LIFE?"

Andre Waters: "I played in lots of big games for the Eagles in the late '80s and early '90s. I'm proud to have been part of that squad. We had one of the greatest defenses ever with Reggie White and Seth Joyner— that whole Gang Green Defense, as they called us. On the other hand, in my early years when I played under head coach Marion Campbell, the Eagles weren't having much success. But on a personal performance basis, I probably have to go back to those early, lean years, back to a transitional year for the Philadelphia Eagles, back to the year that Buddy [Ryan] first came over to the Eagles. That was in 1986. I was selected Defensive Player of the Week for the one and only time in my life. We played the [Los Angeles] Raiders in the game where I won that honor. Personally, that was a pretty unforgettable day, and as I said, it was the first and only time I ever got that award. So I guess I'll pick that game as the most memorable game—the game of my life."

At 5-foot-11 and 194 pounds, Andre Waters was an undersized star on the mean, swarming, aggressive defensive juggernaut that Buddy Ryan assembled in the late '80s and early '90s. He was much criticized as a player who hit hard and sometimes late—a modus operandi that earned him the nickname "Dirty Waters." Andre, born on March 10, 1962, was raised in Florida. In his late teens, he traveled north to little Cheyney University near

Philadelphia to play college ball. Andre left Cheyney undrafted, but scraped his way to a slot on the Eagles' 1984 squad. Within a few years, he became a defensive fixture who managed to lead a squad of All-Pro performers (an honor Andre himself never earned) in tackles.

Andre Waters played 12 years in the NFL. He played a complete decade with the Eagles and followed up with a two-year stint in Arizona to close out his playing career. Andre got into coaching after he hung up his cleats. Sadly, Andre Waters took his own life on November 20, 2006, two weeks after he and I had reminisced about the game of his life.

HOW WELL DO YOU KNOW YOUR BIRDS?

What is the value of home-field advantage? The Eagles have posted a 16-16 overall record in postseason playoff games. Of those 32 postseason games, 17 contests have been played in their own crib in the "friendly" confines of the City of Brotherly Love, in the city whose fans unerringly spell the team's name "E-A-G-L-E-S" while erringly, consistently, and proudly pronouncing it "Iggles." What is the Eagles' record in 17 home-field postseason games?

a) 10-7   b) 8-9   c) 9-8   d) 12-5
e) 14-3   f) 5-12   g) 6-11   h) 4-13

MEET ANDRE WATERS

Along with Dave Pacella (G) and Mike Horan (P), Andre Waters was one of three rookie free agents that reported to the Philadelphia Eagles West Chester University training camp in 1984 and cracked the squad. "As a rookie," Andre confesses, "I was shy and introverted. I had a stammer and I was too self-conscious about my speech impediment to do interviews. I took classes to lose the stammer and, eventually, I got over being so shy."

Andre wasn't a starter as a rookie, but he managed to make his presence felt. "I guess I could pick our game against Washington in 1984

Defensive back Andre Waters watches from the bench as the Eagles battle the New Orleans Saints. Philadelphia won the game 15-13.
Gene Sweeney/Getty Images

as the game of my life, too," Andre suggests. "I ran a kickoff back 89 yards for a game-winning touchdown that day. That was quite a thrill in front of the home crowd. Washington had shut us out 20-0 in the first game we played them that year. To come back later in the season when I was starting to feel more a part of the Eagles and to beat Washington [16-10] with my touchdown really made me feel I could compete in this league."

By 1986, No. 20 had battled his way up to a starting role at strong safety. He displaced Ray Ellis, who was dealt to Cleveland after having held strong safety down for two years. Once installed, Andre was a starter through 1991, splitting duty between strong and free safety.

In his first year as a starter, Andre tied with Mike Reichenbach as the Eagles' top tackler. (Each recorded 129 tackles.) The undersized safety reprised that distinction the following two seasons, 1987 and 1988, and again in 1991. Since defensive luminaries like Reggie White, Jerome Brown, Clyde Simmons, Seth Joyner, Eric Allen, and Wes Hopkins surrounded him, Andre's accomplishment gains in bling.

As the Buddy Ryan defense started to disintegrate after the coach's departure in 1990, Andre's days as an Eagle were numbered. He went to the Arizona Cardinals for his final couple NFL years.

"I guess I have another contender for the game of my life," Andre muses as he reviews his career. "We beat the Giants in 1989 and I scored a TD. That was my other touchdown. I only scored two—the kick return against the Redskins and the fumble recovery against the Giants. Actually, Reggie [White] caused the fumble. He knocked the ball out of [Giants QB Phil Simms'] hand. William Frizzell picked it up and lateraled it to me at about the 3-yard line and I ran it in. That play happened in the same game that Randall [Cunningham] kicked that long punt [91 yards]. But still, being honored as Defensive Player of the Week is hard to top."

As for off-field honors, Andre was awarded the Ed Block Courage Award in 1993. (Each March in Baltimore, the Ed Block Courage Award Foundation honors one player from each team in the NFL who, in the eyes of his teammates, exemplifies a commitment to the principles of sportsmanship and courage.)

Andre briefly mentioned his dissatisfaction with his quest to land an NFL coaching job. His post-NFL playing career started with a coaching position at the University of South Florida, near Andre's home in Tampa. After a couple of years, he was offered a spot in the NFL's minority coaching program. He resigned his college job to accept a summer internship with the St. Louis Rams. The move did not eventuate with an NFL job. His subsequent college jobs were in smaller programs. Even there, Andre said, he ran into coaches who were resentful of him, dismissing him as an ex-NFL big shot who threatened their opportunities. Andre was defensive coordinator for Saint Augustine's College, located in Raleigh, North Carolina, prior to his death.

BUILDING UP TO THE GAME

Buddy Ryan's freshman year as Eagles head coach was anything but smooth. The preseason produced but one win in four decisions. (However, preseason was not a good indicator for Ryan-coached teams. In his entire Eagles tenure, he posted one winning preseason record.) The Birds opened the regular season unconvincingly, getting trounced by the Redskins 41-14. They followed with a heart-breaking but hope-stoking 13-10 loss to the Super Bowl champion Chicago Bears. The Eagles had "Da Bears" tied 10-10 in the final stanza of regulation, only to watch three of their passes get picked off in the final nine minutes. In the overtime period, Eagles return man Charles Crawford fumbled the opening kickoff, and shortly thereafter, Bear Maury Buford booted the game-winning field goal.

Two games later, the 0-3 Birds scored their first victory, a 34-20 win over the L.A. Rams. "I had a big game that day, too, I remember," Andre Waters recalls. "That's definitely another big game that has stayed in my memory bank. I had just won a starting position and our defense had a great day. We held Eric Dickerson real good. [At the time, Dickerson spearheaded the NFL's top rushing offense, but in this contest the Eagles held the former Mustang to 58 yards rushing.] I had an interception and a lot of tackles. I batted some balls down, too. Come to think of it, I had my biggest games that year against the West Coast clubs."

After their victory over the Rams, the Eagles played their finest defensive game of the year. The team's 16-0 whitewash of the Atlanta Falcons (which, by the way, was the game of Garry Cobbs' life) provided a glimpse of the great defenses to come in Philadelphia. Unfortunately, the Birds went into a tailspin after that win. They lost six of the next seven contests, dropping the final four in succession to St. Louis, New York, Detroit, and Seattle. With their season pretty much down the tubes, the team headed out to the West Coast once more, this time to take on the Los Angeles Raiders.

THE GAME OF MY LIFE
NOVEMBER 30, 1986

Andre Waters: "Of course the play I remember best was the fumble recovery. Buddy had us fired up for that game. He was a good coach at getting the best out of a defense. We had lost four straight going into the Raiders game, but even then we could feel something was going to happen with this defense and this team—something good. We knew it was just a matter of time.

"Anyway, it was second-and-six in the overtime period. The Raiders had the ball on our 16. Their quarterback, Jim Plunkett, handed the ball off to Marcus Allen. Marcus was headed right up the middle of the field. The Raiders were trying to set up … a game-winning FG. But that didn't happen! And I give Seth [Joyner] the credit. Seth stripped the ball from Marcus and I just reacted. I saw the ball right in front of me, so all I did was scoop it up. I ran almost the length of the field [81 yards] before I got dragged down around the 4-yard line. [Raider Dokie Williams eventually caught up to Waters and tossed him to the turf.]

"Randall [Cunningham] took it in from the 1-yard line for the W. Like I said, that was a sweet win because we weren't having much success, but you could feel the heart of the team starting to beat. And those Eagles defenses really had heart. We had a bunch of guys who didn't like to lose, and they'd fight you to the death every Sunday in order to beat you—whatever it took. And that's what this game against Los Angeles was. We didn't just give in. We fought to win that game even though we weren't in the running for the playoffs at that point.

"I had a good game personally. I knocked some passes down and had a lot of tackles. I liked to lock up with the Raiders. You know, I was accused of playing the game rough and that's the brand of football the Raiders have been famous for forever, so to come up with a big game against these guys was personally satisfying.

"We played a good game offensively. Randall was really on that day. I think Randall liked to play on the West Coast too. He grew up in Southern California. Of course, Mike Quick was really on that day, too. He caught, what, two, three TD passes? Randall threw a beautiful, long pass to Mike Quick early on and you got the feeling we were going to battle these guys. Then somebody gave us a long punt return for a score, too. [It was Greg Garrity who returned a 76-yard beauty.]

"As I said, that game gave us confidence. It was kind of a jump-start to the great Buddy Ryan Eagles teams a few years later. The Raiders needed a win. They were playing at home. We were playing for pride, and we took them to overtime and then took the game. So a seemingly insignificant game turned out to be pretty important for our team's development. And I was just proud to get the national honor—the Defensive Player of the Week Award—to show that I contributed."

WRAP

As Andre recounts, Randall Cunningham and Mike Quick each turned in outstanding individual performances. Cunningham was 22-39 for 298 yards, three TDs, and one interception. The slender signal-caller also ran 12 times for 59 yards. Meanwhile, Mike Quick caught eight passes for 145 yards and three TDs. Junior Tauralatasi was another effective target that day, catching four tosses for 78 yards.

This game served as a preview of the fine brand of Eagles football that was to follow. The Birds closed out the 1986 season with a tie against the Cardinals, a big victory over Dallas, and a final-game loss. Their '86 log of 5-10-1 improved to 7-8 the following season. And of course, in 1988, having built upon those foundation years, Buddy Ryan's charges won an NFC East crown.

"HOW WELL DO YOU KNOW YOUR BIRDS?" ANSWER
d) 12-5 (From the data provided, math majors may have already derived that their record is 4-11 in games on the road.)

Chapter 23

KEITH JACKSON

"SO, WHAT WAS THE GAME OF YOUR LIFE?"

Keith Jackson: "It was that game against Washington in the beginning of the 1989 season. We were way behind in the first half, but we fought back and won a really exciting game. It was all the more memorable because it happened in Washington in RFK Stadium in front of a hostile crowd."

Keith was an Eagles No. 1 draft choice who was quickly assimilated into the offense. In his debut season, he was chosen for the Pro Bowl. The Sporting News *selected him Rookie of the Year. In four productive seasons with the Birds, Keith grabbed 242 passes for 2,756 yards and 20 touchdowns. Currently, he's in Arizona working for a youth organization named Park Positive Atmosphere, which Keith launched while still playing in Philly. Park Positive Atmosphere is an after-school program for underachieving students ranging from eighth to 12th grades.*

HOW WELL DO YOU KNOW YOUR BIRDS?

The Jackson Four: can you name the four Jacksons who have caught passes as Eagles?

MEET KEITH JACKSON

Keith Jerome Jackson was born April 19, 1965, and raised in Little Rock, Arkansas. His football prowess led him to the University of Oklahoma. In the Sooners' run-oriented offense, he caught only 62 passes for 1,470 yards in a four-year collegiate career. He earned All-America laurels in '86. His physical attributes—6-foot-2, 250 pounds with good speed—made him a prized commodity in the 1988 draft.

"At the NFL combine, Buddy Ryan told me the Eagles [who picked 13th that year] planned to pick me if I was still around when their turn came," Keith says. "Green Bay drafted ahead of the Eagles. They told me they were interested in me, but they ended up drafting Sterling Sharpe instead. So I became an Eagle—a first-round pick. For years, Eric Allen joked with me about all the money I cost him! The Eagles were set to draft him first, but they changed that plan when I was still available. As it was, Eric was available in the second round and they drafted him then.

"I'll never forget coming to Philly—the day I came to Philly. Most teams send a limo to pick the guys up, but when I flew into Philadelphia for the first time for the draft announcement, Jerome Brown and Keith Byars picked me at the airport. They said they were excited I was joining the team. I thought that was a great gesture, to have my new teammates greet me. The three of us got to be good friends. [At the time, the Eagles seemed to be following a Keith-Jerome drafting strategy/pattern: in '86, the No. 1 pick was Keith Byars; in '87, it was Jerome Brown; and in '88, it was Keith Jerome Jackson.]

"Then, when I went to my first Eagles camp, Buddy Ryan was already telling the press that I was the starting tight end instead of John Spagnola, who had held the job a few years. [Spagnola started at tight end from '84 to '87.] So coming to Philly was exciting."

Number 88 spent four seasons in Quaker City before exercising his rights under free agency and shoving off to Miami. Keith's first Dolphins season was a virtual replication of his final season in Philly. (He had 48 receptions both years, gaining 569 receiving yards in '92 as a Bird versus 594 yards as a Dolphin.)

After three seasons in Miami, Keith headed to Green Bay, where he waged his two final campaigns before changing careers.

Tight end Keith Jackson celebrates a 27-21 victory over the Los Angeles Rams on September 23, 1990. *Stephen Dunn/Getty Images*

BUILDING UP TO THE GAME

Going into the 1988 season, the Eagles were coming off the fabled Fog Bowl in Chicago, which dropped the curtain on the '87 season. In the '89 exhibition season, the team went 4-1—the best preseason mark a Buddy Ryan Eagles team ever registered. The Birds seemed hungry and poised to rocket to the Super Bowl for the first time sine 1980. The city of Philadelphia was all the more pumped up over its powerhouse team after the opener, when the Birds blew out the Seattle Seahawks 31-7. The following week, they headed down to Washington for a showdown with the always-tough 'Skins. Washington had won the Super Bowl two years earlier, trouncing John Elway's Denver Broncos convincingly, 42-10. However, the Redskins were slipping and looking to turn things around against the Birds. On game day, 53,493 whooping Redskin fans filled RFK Stadium, ready to reclaim their glory.

THE GAME OF MY LIFE
SEPTEMBER 17, 1989

Keith Jackson: "We fell behind fast. [Washington scored on its first two offensive plays from scrimmage.] We couldn't get anything going in the first quarter, but we never panicked. I seem to recall that Washington got the lead up to 20 points. [Actually, Washington led by 20 twice in the first half.]

"But the second half was a different story. The offense really started to click. Randall was really hot. He had a great day. So did I. I caught three touchdown passes [of 17, 5, and 4 yards]. A couple other guys caught TD passes, too. [Mike Quick caught one, as did Cris Carter—to the possible dismay of Buddy Ryan, who eventually shipped Carter off to a probable Hall of Fame career in Minnesota with the quip, 'All he does is catch touchdown passes.']

"Eagles fans probably remember the end of that game. Washington had the ball with just a little time [1:16 minutes] left. Then their big back, Gerald Riggs, fumbled and Wes Hopkins recovered it, ran it back, and we got the ball inside the 5. [Washington center Rawley McKenzie accidentally poked the ball out of Riggs' arms and Al Harris picked it up. When Washington tackle Jim Lachey was bringing Harris down, Wes Hopkins took a lateral and rumbled 77 yards to the 4-yard line before Rickey Sanders stopped his advance.]

"We got the ball and Randall threw me a short [4-yard] TD pass for the win. Randall had a great way of thinking out there. He was always looking for matchups, like trying to isolate a 4.4 guy like Keith Byars on a linebacker who runs a 4.9. If I ever got a mismatch, I figured the ball was headed my way."

WRAP

It was a huge day for quarterback Randall Cunningham, who completed 34 of 46 passes for 447 yards, five TDs, and one interception. Cunningham set a single-game club record both for completions and yardage. After the game, he revealed that he had signed a five-year contract extension earlier that day that would keep him in Eagle green through 1995.

"HOW WELL DO YOU KNOW YOUR BIRDS?" ANSWER
Harold Jackson (215 passes from 1969-1972)
Keith Jackson (242 passes from 1988-1991)
Kenny Jackson (118 passes from 1984-1988 and 1990)
Randy Jackson (two passes in 1974)

(And yes, the Eagles come oh-so-close to boasting a bona fide Jackson Five. If only T.J. Jackson, an undrafted wide receiver/defensive back from Illinois, had caught a pass. T.J. played three games for the 1966 Eagles, but never got his mitts on an aerial. He played a little difense and returned kicks.)

Chapter 24

SETH JOYNER

"SO, WHAT WAS THE GAME OF YOUR LIFE?"

Seth Joyner: "The game that first comes to my mind is that Monday night game we won in Houston at the House of Pain. It was an important game in front of a national audience. We needed a win to stay in the playoff race. I was sick that night. I wasn't myself at all, but I ended up playing one of the best games of my life."

Like Chuck Bednarik, Bill Bergey, Maxie Baughan, Jerry Robinson, and William Thomas, Seth Joyner is one of the all-time Eagles linebacking greats. Seth was a two-time Pro Bowler and two-time Eagles Defensive MVP. His intensity and savage physical play immortalized him with Iggles faithful.

HOW WELL DO YOU KNOW YOUR BIRDS?

Reggie White is the all-time sack leader for the Eagles. Defensive linemen occupy the first five slots on that list. The first linebacker appears in the No. 6 position on the all-time sack list. Who is he?

a) Seth Joyner
b) William Thomas
c) Jeremiah Trotter
d) Bill Romanowski
e) Byron Evans
f) Mike Reichenbach
g) Garry Cobb
h) Jerry Robinson
i) Bill Bergey
j) Frank LeMaster

MEET SETH JOYNER

Seth Joyner was born November 18, 1964, in Spring Valley, New York, where he starred as a gridder. He trekked the length of the country to play his college football at Texas-El Paso. He was an eighth-round draft choice, but his intensity and physical skills earned him a slot on the Eagles roster. Coach Buddy Ryan was also in his rookie season. Not only did he keep Seth on the roster, he also gave the young prospect seven starts his first year. Seth shared the right linebacker position that season with Alonzo Johnson, a second-round 1986 draftee from Florida. The following season, Seth shifted to starting left linebacker—a position he nailed down through 1993. The 6-foot-2, 240-pound athlete blossomed into a vital member of Philly's feared Gang Green defense—a defense that is acknowledged as one of the NFL's all-time finest.

In '87, his first season as a full-time starter, Seth was the team's third leading tackler, ahead of veterans like Reggie White, Clyde Simmons, and Garry Cobb. In Joyner's Eagles career, he played 120 games, was twice selected as the Eagles Most Valuable Defensive Player (1991, 1992) and twice selected for the Pro Bowl. In 1991, he was chosen All-Pro. Three times in his career, No. 59 was honored as the Defensive Player of the Week.

Seth was a spirited locker-room motivator and a team spokesmen. His blue-collar style endeared him to the hometowners. After departing from the Eagles, Seth played with a number of other teams, including the Cardinals, Packers, and Broncos.

Seth now lives in Arizona. He has parlayed his media savvy into a postseason career, serving as NFL analyst for a variety of TV and radio networks.

BUILDING UP TO THE GAME

The year 1991 was a strange one in the Quaker City. On January 8, owner Norman Braman did not renew Buddy Ryan's contract. Instead, he promoted Rich Kotite to head coach. Kotite had been serving as the team's offensive coordinator.

Seth Joyner (No. 59) reaches out for a sack against Green Bay quarterback Brett Favre. *Jonathan Daniel/Getty Images*

Under its new mentor, Philadelphia went 4-1 in a rare winning exhibition season. The Eagles started the season 3-1—the team's finest start since 1981, the year that followed their 1980 Super Bowl appearance. The Birds achieved this early-season success despite losing quarterback Randall Cunningham for the season in the opener against Green Bay. Jim McMahon substituted effectively, but McMahon too went down in game five, which precipitated a four-game losing streak. Pressing four different quarterbacks into service in eight games contributed heavily to the Birds' uncharacteristic 3-5 midseason record. The proud, battle-savvy Birds veterans mounted a surge at that point, They rolled to successive victories over the Giants, Browns, Bengals, and Cards.

At that point, the resurgent Philadelphians headed to the House of Pain for a Monday night shootout with the Oilers. A Philadelphia victory was essential to keep their playoff hopes alive. The Birds were at an emotional peak—with the exception of one key member.

"I was miserable all day, feeling weak and sick," Seth Joyner recalls. "I rested all day long. When game time came around, about the only thing our training staff could do was rub me down with alcohol in the locker room just to try to get my fever down. I had a fever of about 104, I think. They tried to talk me out of playing, but I wasn't going to miss that game."

As for Houston, they entered the fray at 9-3. They were contending fiercely for the Central Division title. If they won, it would be their first title since the AFL-NFL merger in 1970. Most important, Houston needed a win to secure home-field advantage throughout the playoffs.

THE GAME OF MY LIFE
DECEMBER 2, 1991

Seth Joyner: "My energy level was never lower for a football game. I was taking a knee … whenever I heard the whistle blow. I was trying to conserve what little energy I had. Byron Evans was calling the first- and second-down defensive plays so I didn't have to hustle back to the huddle. If I stayed on the field for third down, I'd make the call, but I felt so weak that day. Whenever I went off the field, my teammates would come out on to the field and help me over to the sidelines. …

"You'd never know how sick I felt from the statistics. Statistically, as I recall, I think I had 10 tackles, two sacks, two forced fumbles, two recovered fumbles, and one interception. Not only that, I dropped what would have been another sure interception. I had it right in my hands, but dropped it.

"I kind of amazed myself that day. Haywood Jeffires, on one play, ran a slant from the slot position. I stayed right with him. I mean, 15 yards downfield I was all over him! Haywood could really run too, but I was just in the zone that day. A couple of times I remember basically running over Bruce Matthews to get to Warren Moon. Bruce was one of the premier linemen in the league for years. I had two sacks, but on a couple of other plays I got to Warren Moon just as he was releasing the ball. When Warren got up, he was kind of looking around like, 'Where'd that guy come from? How'd he get in here so deep so fast? Who's supposed to be keeping him out?'

"It was probably the most intimidating, dominating game by a defense that I've ever seen—even more than that Body Bag game in Washington. 'Cause it wasn't just me having a great defensive day out there. Our whole team was hitting. We were in the House of Pain and we wanted to intimidate. We had a special challenge that night. The Oilers offense played finesse football with that run and shoot system they used. Our D was not based on finesse. We played a physical game. We just hit anything that moved, and all our guys played extremely physical that night. Wes Hopkins, he caught Ernest Givens with one forearm. Wow! And guys like Andre Waters were hitting people all over the field.

"After the game, I was so drained! … Since that was the Monday night game, we only had a short week to get ready for the next game. The following Sunday we drove up to New York. I still didn't feel good, but I wound up having another great game. I could never figure all that out, but that's what happened, especially in that Houston game—I played the game of my life."

WRAP

The account in the *New York Times* the following day read: "Who needs an offense? Not the Philadelphia Eagles, as long as they have Seth Joyner and the National Football League's best defense. … The story for

Philadelphia was the play of Joyner, the often-overlooked linebacker in a defense featuring Reggie White and the game's best front four."

The Joyner-led defense forced five fumbles and deprived Houston of a touchdown for the first time in more than two years.

Quarterback Jim McMahon was in the lineup, but the Eagles offense couldn't get untracked. The halftime score was 3-0 in favor of Houston, thanks to a 42-yard Al Del Greco three-pointer as the first-half clock ran out. In the second half, McMahon was knocked out of the contest when he hyperextended the elbow on his throwing arm early in the third quarter. Jeff Kemp replaced him and tossed a 24-yard TD pass to Keith Jackson a short time after Philadelphia's Roger Ruzek had kicked a 23-yard field goal to knot the score at 3-3. That TD turned out to be the difference. It was the game's sole six-pointer. As for the Ruzek field goal, not surprisingly, it was set up by Seth Joyner's recovery of Warren Moon's fumbled center snap. Seth scooped up the ball and advanced it 3 yards to the 8-yard line. Three straight Eagles passes failed to find their mark before Ruzek delivered on a short field goal.

Kemp finished the game at QB, connecting on 10 of 17 passing attempts for 84 yards. The TD pass was Kemp's first since being cut by the Seattle Seahawks. Almost as important as his TD toss, however, Kemp led a fourth-quarter drive that consumed 10:05 of the game clock. The drive was consummated with a Ruzek 29-yard field goal. Those points made victory a two-score proposition for the Oilers with only 3:52 left to accomplish the task against an unbudging defense.

The Oilers did manage a threat at the end. They reached the Philadelphia 24-yard line in the final seconds, but Warren Moon's three passes into the end zone hit the turf.

In the final tally, Joyner and his defensive mates limited the Houston offensive juggernaut to 239 yards—significantly below the 362 yards per game they had been averaging.

Houston fell to 9-4, but went on to win the Central Division title rather easily. Their Super Bowl hopes were dashed when Denver eliminated them 26-24 in the AFC Divisional playoff game.

As for the Birds, they continued their torrid win streak. The following Sunday, they bested the Giants at the Meadowlands. The still-sick Seth Joyner was again stellar. However, the team's dream drive sputtered to a disappointing halt the following week when Dallas topped the Birds at the Vet. The Eagles 10-6 record, though not good enough to make the playoffs, distinguished Philadelphia as the only team, along with San Francisco, with 10 or more wins in each of the previous four seasons. And the Eagles D? They became only the fifth defense in NFL history to rank No. 1 in fewest yards versus the run, fewest yards versus the pass, and fewest yards allowed overall.

Looking back at that Houston game, Seth Joyner sums up: "It's still amazes me. As bad as I felt physically, it was statistically the best game I ever played. I got the Defensive Player of the Week Award when I was having trouble just standing up. All I can say is it was kind of surreal being out there on the field feeling that bad. I felt almost oblivious to things. Usually I'm intense on the field, but I was too sick to have my normal intensity. But what a game it turned out to be!"

"HOW WELL DO YOU KNOW YOUR BIRDS?" ANSWER
a) Seth Joyner (With 37.5 sacks, he leads the linebacker pack for all-time sacks as an Eagle. The only other linebacker who cracks the top 20 is William Thomas with 33 sacks.)

Chapter 25

VAI SIKAHEMA

"SO, WHAT WAS THE GAME OF YOUR LIFE?"

Vai Sikahema: "There were lots of great games in this town. I've seen hundreds both from the field and as a broadcaster. But if we're talking about the most memorable game I had wearing that No. 22 on my back, it's pretty hard not to pick that game against the Giants when I ran the punt back for a TD."

It took Vai but two seasons in Eagle green to immortalize himself to Philly fans. Vai's outgoing personality seemingly connected with the totality of the Iggles fan base, broad and confusing though it may be. Vai was as popular with staid, posh Main Liners as he was with raucous 700-level screamers. Philadelphians will never shake (nor seek to shake) their kinship with Rocky Balboa and underdogs in general. (Eagles fans cannot only say Invincible *now, they can spell it with the same certainty that they spell E-A-G-L-E-S.) Vai struck the same chord with Philly fans that Tommy McDonald struck three decades earlier. Both men were about 5-foot-9 or thereabouts— Lilliputians in a land of Brobdingnagians. (That means they were little guys in a land of giants, if you're not too Swift-oriented; i.e., if you don't remember the Cliff Notes from Jonathon Swift's* Gulliver's Travels.) *McDonald tipped the scales gently at about 170 pounds, give or (most likely) take 10 pounds. Vai weighed in at about 190 pounds, McDonald's approximate weight extrapolated into more contemporary times. Neither guy was a flat-out speed burner. Like McDonald, Vai's forte was agility, balance, and dogged determination rather than pedal-to-the-metal speed.*

HOW WELL DO YOU KNOW YOUR BIRDS?

Which Eagles punt returner recorded the highest total number of fair catches in a single NFL season? His total of 33 that year tops the No. 2 guy on the list by a whopping seven fair catches.

a) Vai Sikahema   b) Timmy Brown
c) Jerry Norton   d) Brian Mitchell
e) Tommy McDonald   f) Reno Mahe
g) Bill Bradley   h) Wally Henry

MEET VAI SIKAHEMA

Born August 29, 1962, Vai Sikahema was the first native of Tonga to play in the NFL. That might strike you as an entry for your Captain Obvious notebook, but hold on. Vai is not the *only* Tonga native who lists the NFL on his resumé. Alfred Pupunu was also born in that faraway land. So was Deuce Lutui, a 6-foot-4, 330-pound former USC lineman now beefing up the Cardinals' roster. Deuce happens to be Vai's cousin. But wait, that's not all … Vai's family tree boasts another NFL-er: cousin Reno Mahe, current Eagles special teamer. So much for Captain Obvious.

Tonga is practically a football factory. They've produced more NFL players than my high school, Father Judge, in Northeast Philly—and Judge has won a few city football titles.

When Vai was seven, his family left Tonga and settled in Mesa, Arizona. There, Vai starred on the high school grid. "I was set to play at Arizona State under Frank Kush," Vai recalls, "but then Kush got himself into a bit of a situation. One of his players accused Frank of punching him. Kush was removed from the head coaching job. So instead of ASU, I wound up going to BYU, which turned out to be a very positive move for me. Who knows what would have happened if I had gone to ASU?"

Vai Sikahema played the game of his life on November 22, 1992, against the New York Giants. *Bill Hickey/Getty Images*

It was as a BYU running back and kick return specialist that Vai Sikahema first caught fans' attention. In the 1980 Holiday Bowl, he returned a punt for a touchdown in BYU's exciting 46-45 come-from-behind victory over Southern Methodist. In his sophomore season, Vai placed fourth in the Western Athletic Conference in punt returns, averaging 8.6 yards on 44 returns. At that point, he took a hiatus from his college career and headed to South Dakota to serve as a missionary for the Church of the Latter Day Saints (or Mormons).

He rejoined the Cougars grid squad in '84. Behind Steve Young, BYU won the national championship that year. The Tongan kid wasn't completely overshadowed. He garnered some national attention of his own that season. Vai was Honorable Mention All-WAC and ranked seventh nationally in kickoff returns. In his senior year, he made second-team All-WAC as a returner and closed his college career out with more punt returns than any other Cougar in the school's history.

Vai was the 254th player selected in the '86 draft, when the Cardinals nabbed him in the 10th round. He made the Phoenix squad and quickly distinguished himself as one of the game's craftiest punt returners, twice earning invitations to the Pro Bowl (1987, 1988). In the '87 game, Vai set the NFL Pro-Bowl single-game punt-return record with seven in one game. Incidentally, Eagle Reggie White was the MVP of that game on the strength of his four sacks.

Vai was subsequently dealt to Green Bay, where he spent a year prior to heading to Philly. He quickly became a Vet Stadium favorite, thrilling crowds with his gutsy, gritty style. He was gutsy and gritty enough to earn a coveted slot on the 1992 All-Madden Team—the ultimate measure of the no-fear philosophy conferred, ironically, by a guy who crisscrosses the country in his bus due to his fear of flying.

Vai called it quits after the '93 season, but not without leaving a lasting footprint on the NFL. He ended his pro football career ranked No. 1 all time in career punt returns. (He is now at No. 4—Brian Mitchell perches comfortably atop the current heap.) Twice Vai led the league in total yards gained on punts in a season. Only one other player, Alvin Hammond, has ever bettered that accomplishment. Hammond led the league in this category one more time than Vai. At one point, Sikahema also ranked second in career punt-return yardage. (He's still in the top five.)

Upon retirement, Vai Sikahema cashed in on the media career he had nurtured in his playing years. As an active player, his media resumé was surprisingly extensive. Way back in 1986 as a rookie with the Phoenix Cardinals, Vai not only pursued his education (he earned a communications degree from BYU in 2002), but also launched his TV career at KSAZ-TV in Arizona. He spent four years at KSAZ, where he oftentimes shared the anchor desk. After he was dealt to the Packers in 1991, he continued in media as a sports reporter for WFRV-TV in Green Bay, Wisconsin.

After retiring from the Eagles, the rolling-stone-like kick returner (referring to his running style, not necessarily his musical taste) gathered no moss. In April 1994, he joined WCAU full time. In December 2005, he expanded his responsibilities to include weeknight sports director/anchor at Philly's WB 17 News at 10. He and his wife, Keala, live in South Jersey. They have three sons and a daughter.

BUILDING UP TO THE GAME

The Eagles went into the '92 season reeling from a couple of personnel losses. All-Pro defensive tackle Jerome Brown had been killed in a car accident on June 25, a month before training camp. The big defensive lineman was speeding on a wet Florida road when he lost control of his car. Neither he nor the sole passenger, his 12-year-old nephew, was wearing a seat belt. Both were killed as a result of the crash.

Meanwhile, tight end Keith Jackson, another frequent All-Pro, invoked his rights as a free agent and inked a Miami contract. Adding to these woes, starting left defensive tackle Mike Pitts, who tallied 100 tackles and two sacks the previous year, suffered a pinched nerve in his lower back. Nonetheless, following a less-than-promising 2-3 preseason, the Eagles burst out of the gates like gangbusters. They squeaked by the Saints 15-13 in the opener before galloping out to a 4-0 record. Then the bubble burst. They slumped, winning only two of the next half-dozen games. The offense was so sluggish that head coach Buddy Ryan benched three-time All-Pro QB Randall Cunningham for a couple games and inserted the gung-ho Jim McMahon.

A faltering flock of Birds entered the Meadowlands on November 22, 1992, to take on the New York Giants. Philadelphia's rivals up the Jersey turnpike were itching for revenge. The Giants hadn't beaten the

Eagles since their 1990 home opener, and 68,153 fans piled into the Meadowlands eager—and vociferous—to extract their revenge from the slumping Eagles.

THE GAME OF MY LIFE
NOVEMBER 22, 1992

Vai Sikahema: "It was one of those raw, cold New York days in early winter. The contest turned into a marathon for the guys on the field. [Vai's right: the game was an excruciating three-hour and 42-minute drenching affair.] The game had lots of big plays. Early in the game, I had a kickoff return of 41 yards. Randall had been reinserted into the lineup at that point and we had a long drive [a 46-yarder] that ended with a TD toss to Herschel Walker. Roger Ruzek missed the extra point and we got pretty far behind. [Eventually, the Eagles found themselves on the wrong side of a 20-6 ledger.] But then we really started to perform on both sides of the ball.

"I remember Keith Byars picking one of Randall's passes clean off his shoe tops. I had a decent return [39 yards] to start that drive, and then, as I said, Keith closed it out with that pretty catch for the score. Everybody seemed to catch fire once we got rolling. Herschel Walker also scored one for us [Herschel scored on an 11-yard scamper], and Heath Sherman [who ended the day with 109 yards on 17 carries] ran a long one in for a [30-yard] score. On defense, Seth Joyner intercepted one and took it [43 yards] to the house.

"It was in the third or fourth quarter, later in the game—I can hardly remember. There was so much happening in that game. I went back to receive a punt, and it was one of those fortunate times when I had plenty of room to catch it. I made a couple of moves and headed down the sideline. I remember I had to cut back on the punter, Sean Landeta, and Sean tore out his knee. He ended up missing the rest of the season. After that, I only had one other guy to get by. That was Jesse Campbell. I remember Jesse because he had been in our training camp that year till the last cut. After he was cut, the Giants picked him up. Jesse was a safety. Anyway, I outran him to the corner."

"On my way back to the bench, out of the corner of my eye, I caught a glimpse of the goal post wrapped in protective padding. Just for a moment, it reminded me of the heavy bag I used to work out on with my father. My dad didn't know much about football. When I was a kid, he wanted me to be a boxer, and we trained on a heavy bag. So I have no idea what made me do this—you know, this took place way before the era of stashing cell phones away for pre-planned end zone celebrations—but I ran over and started punching the bag. It was instinctive, unpremeditated—just fun. But the big reason was that I knew my dad would be watching the game back in Arizona, and, well, I really did it for him. I knew he'd get a kick out of it.

"I really didn't give it much thought after that. Things went great for us. We staged a huge comeback. My TD helped the cause. We wound up beating the Giants 47-34, so the cold rain and crummy weather didn't faze us. Actually, it was the most points ever scored against the Giants at the Meadowlands till that time. After the game, a couple of Eagles marketing guys came running over to me, telling me, 'That was brilliant, Vai! To think of that in a split second—to make the connection between Philly and Philly fighters and Rocky and Joe Frazier and tie in all that Philly boxing legacy with one move. A stroke of genius!' I had no idea about any of that. I was just sending a little message out to my dad in Arizona.

"I remember our trip back down the turnpike after the game. When the team bus stopped, I called my wife to ask if my dad had seen the game. She said he had already called three times. He loved it! The amazing part about the whole thing is that it really helped my post-NFL broadcasting career. The people at Channel 10 mentioned it right off the bat in our first conversation about joining their broadcast team. In the publicity campaign they aired when I came on board, they showed me punching the goal post and a lot of other different footage and played 'My Vai' to the tune of 'My Guy,' that old Mary Wells song. Anyway, the whole incident helped open doors. And you can't believe how many people still come up to me and tell me they were there and saw the whole thing live … at the Vet or Yankee Stadium."

WRAP

The older we get, the faster we are. Vai has to beware that little universal truth as he ages. It's quite possible that when Vai rolls that punching bag tale out to future generations of Sikahemas, the story could take on, let's say, more grandiose tones. Maybe future versions will have him toppling the goal post with one punch. Or maybe Vai's great-grandkids will be telling school chums how Mike Tyson called Vai after the game to tell Vai they couldn't pay Iron Mike enough money to climb into a ring with Vai.

Of course, that's speculation. What is not speculation is that the key opportunities in Vai's life seem to revolve around punches. Because of a Frank Kush punch, Vai wound up at BYU, where he benefited from the national exposure of playing on a national championship team. Then, a few years later, Vai's goal post punches helped him land a successful broadcasting position. If good things come in threes, what's next? Perhaps Howard Eskine shouldn't challenge Vai so often when the two team up (or square off) on the sports wrap on Sunday nights. Punch number three might land Vai a job as Philly mayor. (Just kidding, Howard.)

"HOW WELL DO YOU KNOW YOUR BIRDS?" ANSWER

d) Brian Mitchell (Brian is the all-time career leader for fair catches with 217. The gap between Mitchell and the second man on the list, Tim Brown—Oakland's Tim Brown, not No. 22 for the Eagles in the '60s—is 67 fair catches!)

Chapter 26

DAVID ALEXANDER

"SO, WHAT WAS THE GAME OF YOUR LIFE?"

David Alexander: "That's tough to pick. We sure had some memorable games back in those days, like the Fog Bowl in Chicago. Who could ever forget that one? Of course, that particular game wasn't my best game, nor was it the Eagles' finest hour, but it certainly is a day I'll never forget. Then we had that series of games against Dallas: the Bounty Bowl, Bounty Bowl II, and the Porkchop Bowl. Dallas was rebuilding in those days, and we usually had our way with them during that stretch. The team that seemed to give us fits was the Redskins. We had trouble figuring Joe Gibbs out. So I think that has to be my answer. When I look back, I think if you ask me what the game of my life was, I'd have to say it was the day we beat the 'Skins at the end of the 1992 season. That was an exciting game—tense and dramatic. And the win put us back into the playoffs after not being in them the year before."

From an anonymous, middle-round draft pick, David Alexander persevered and eventually centered the Eagles offensive line for five straight seasons during which he never missed a game or a snap. Coach Buddy Ryan honored Dave by appointing him team co-captain along with Randall Cunningham. In all, Dave played 131 games in the NFL trenches. He played 112 consecutively.

HOW WELL DO YOU
KNOW YOUR BIRDS?

Which guy on this list was *not* a winner of the Eagles Offensive or Defensive MVP Award for three consecutive years?

a) Randall Cunningham   b) Donovan McNabb
c) Reggie White   d) William Thomas

MEET DAVID ALEXANDER

David Alexander was born July 28, 1964, in Silver Springs, Maryland. He spent his high school days in Broken Arrow, Oklahoma. There, as a 6-foot-3, 215 pounder, he earned All-State football recognition at Broken Arrow High. After graduation, Dave relocated to Tulsa to compete at the collegiate level. There, he was a four-year football letterman and three-year starter. During his collegiate days, he displayed his versatility by switching positions on the offensive line. He performed regardless of where he lined up. That versatility would stand him in good stead upon reaching the pros.

The former Broken Arrow star redshirted the '82 season in order to bulk up. As a 240-pound freshman the following campaign, he started at tackle. Unfortunately, he suffered an ankle injury in the second game, and his season came to a premature halt.

Undeterred, he resurfaced with gusto the following year, becoming the only sophomore to crack the first-team offense on the All-Missouri Valley Conference team. Shifted from offensive tackle to guard in '85, he reprised the honor. He also earned Honorable Mention, All-America honors. Dave was invited to the East-West Shrine Game as well as the Senior Bowl at the conclusion of his college career.

David drew sufficient NFL attention for the Eagles to draft him in the fifth round. Shortly after he arrived at the Eagles training camp as a rookie, Dave was summoned to report to offensive line coach Bill Walsh. Fearing he had already been cut without playing a single down ("What did I know?" David says, smiling at his own naiveté), he was set at ease when Walsh told him he was shifting to tackle. The move was

---

Offensive lineman David Alexander watches the Eagles gain a 40-8 victory over the 49ers on October 2, 1994. *Otto Greule Jr./Getty Images*

necessitated by an injury to Ken Reeves, a veteran who had alternated between starting left guard and starting left tackle in '86. "I kind of stretched the truth," David confesses. "I told Bill I knew the playbook for tackles, but I didn't. It didn't matter. I picked it up quick enough. I'd have done anything to make the squad."

The Eagles offensive line was overhauled in 1987. Tom Jelesky, Nick Haden, and Leonard Mitchell—starters on the 1986 offensive line—were replaced by Adam Schreiber, Gerry Feehery, and Joe Conwell. Dave became the ever-ready lineman, ready to fill in at any offensive line position at any time. Number 72 wound up playing all five offensive line positions that season.

In '88, Dave started at left guard. The following year, he was repositioned to center, where he held dominion till 1995. By 1993, Dave Alexander had snapped the ball on 2,397 consecutive plays. His string was broken when he was given a break in a meaningless game.

BUILDING UP TO THE GAME

David Alexander recalls, "This was a big game, a decisive game for us. At that point in the season with only two games left to play, we were in a three-way race in our conference. Dallas was out ahead by two games and they weren't playing that week till Monday night. Washington and us had identical 19-5 records coming into the game. Dallas was 11-3. Whoever won our game was assured a playoff spot, and they'd still have a chance—admittedly, a small chance—to win the division. Dallas would have to lose both its final two games for that to happen, but hey, that '92 Eagles squad was a veteran team that knew that in football, anything can happen. ... The big thing as far as we were concerned was this: if we beat Washington, we're in the playoffs."

THE GAME OF MY LIFE
DECEMBER 20, 1992

David Alexander: "I can talk about the Washington game easier in reverse. The whole game boiled down to one last play. Washington had the ball on the 5-yard line with two seconds left. It probably looked strange to any observer, but I was sitting on the bench at that point when the whole stadium was on its feet. ... The whole Eagles bench was standing on its feet along the sidelines. But I had this superstition about sitting in the same spot on the bench every time I was not on the field, so when all this drama was unfolding, that's where I was! I couldn't even really see the final play. I was trying to catch it on the Jumbotron, the big screen, whatever it was called in those days. Those big stadium screens weren't nearly as good back in those days as they are now. Anyway the 'Skins QB, Mark Rypien, lofted the ball to their big-play receiver, No. 84, Gary Clark. But at the last second, Eric Allen stepped in front of Gary and batted the ball away. Eric's play got us back into the playoffs! I felt good for our coach, Rich Kotite, 'cause Rich had taken over the year before and we missed the playoffs. So this W was sweet for him. And the Vet crowd! I played a lot of games at the Vet, but I never, ever heard that place as loud as it was after Eric swatted that one away. The place simply erupted!

"The game was emotional start to finish for us. Another thing I'll always remember is Brian Baldinger that day. I didn't get a chance to play too much with Brian, but was he ever pumped up! He was running up and down the bench screaming at everybody, picking up the whole offensive line—especially after Heath Sherman ran for that first-half score.

"Hey, look, I said I was gonna talk about the game in reverse. Can you blame me with a finish like that? Anyway, that first-half running TD that Heath scored is what had Brian so pumped up. You know, for a lineman, the pro game is all about pass blocking, but that's not the way you come up as a kid. When you first start playing football, line play is all about run blocking. Because that's the first thing you learn how to do, I think a lineman always gets a bigger thrill deep down out of blocking for the run. Well, that's what we did a lot of that day. We really moved the ball on the ground against the 'Skins. That was gratifying because they had a tough D with quality players like Dave Butz and Andre Collins. So the run that Heath scored on felt as great for the guys on the line as it did for Heath. It was a play we called a '31'—nothing fancy, just a simple run between center and left guard. Brian and I worked together on that one. [Sherman's march took place in the first half. It was the Birds' only first-half score. They went to the locker room trailing Washington 10-7.]

"So we were trailing at the end of the first half, but that game—I don't know—we just had confidence and never doubted ourselves. Even though we were down, I don't think any of us thought we would lose the game, and one of the main reasons we didn't was the way we established the run and the success we had on the ground. We kept pounding the ball at them all day. The offensive line did a nice job and eventually swung the momentum our way. … Yeah, I have a lot of wonderful memories playing for this team, but that game, I think that might be the top."

WRAP

True to David Alexander's account, Heath Sherman played a key role in the victory. All told, Sherman plowed through the Washington D for 98 yards on 18 carries. The Eagles, led mostly by Heath Sherman, won the ground war 160 yards to 118. Their running game set up the final points, a 23-yard Roger Ruzek field goal with 3:35 left. The Ruzek kick forced Washington to go for a TD rather than a field goal on its final, desperation drive.

The Eagles defense was Johnny-on-the-spot all afternoon. They picked off two crucial Rypien passes in addition to Allen's game-ender. Obviously, the Allen pick saved the day, but the other two INTs were crucial as well. Before each pick, the 'Skins were in field goal position.

In contrast, the pass offense was sluggish all day and never got untracked. QB Randall Cunningham was not at the height of his game. He closed the contest a statistically pedestrian 13 of 24 for 149 yards.

The first Eagles score of the second half came in the third quarter on a nifty Cunningham completion to Calvin Williams, who had broken free in the end zone. "The play, as I recall, was an audible," said the Eagles QB after the game. "We were having so much success moving the ball on the ground that when I saw the defense sneaking up, I changed the play." The play happened to work, but not because the 'Skins were crossed up. Cunningham had to toss that particular 28-yard scoring flip into double coverage. Randall heaped praise on Calvin Williams for the catch. "I got the ball out there so Calvin had to make a play to bring it down, and that's just what he did," Cunningham noted.

One of the more astute observations on the final-play action came from recently acquired Eagles backup receiver Roy Green. Green confessed that he knew what play the 'Skins were running when they broke the huddle for that final play. "They ran a scat dodge, that was their call, and I thought it was a beauty to pick," said Green. Green spoke with insider knowledge. A few of the Redskins' offensive coaches were with the Cardinals at the same time as Green. "When they got to Washington, those guys were still using basically the same system I had played under, so I recognized what they were running as soon as they broke the huddle. I thought the play choice was pretty solid because it gave the QB three options. He could hit a back in the flat, a receiver in the corner, or a receiver dragging in the middle of the zone defense. They're all terrific options against the blitz or anything else the defense throws up."

Green had the play figured out minus one detail: All-Pro Eric Allen happened to be patrolling the defensive backfield. And that's who saved the game and the Eagles' season in one unforgettable moment.

"HOW WELL DO YOU KNOW YOUR BIRDS?" ANSWER
b) Donovan McNabb (Cunningham and White each won from 1987-1989; Thomas won from 1995-1997.)

Chapter 27

BRIAN BALDINGER

"SO, WHAT WAS THE GAME OF YOUR LIFE?"

Brian Baldinger: "Wow, that's a tough one to pick. My whole first season in Philly was special, really special. First of all, on a personal basis, I was just arriving in town and I got a chance to find out quick how special the city of Philadelphia was. The way the fans love this team is something really special. Then Jerome Brown had that horrible accident and the team dedicated the season to him. So several games that year stick out. The 'Skins game was huge. We clinched a playoff spot by beating them in our next-to-last game of the regular season. Of course, Washington had won the Super Bowl over Buffalo the year before. So it was a meaningful win for us, all the more so because the season before, the Eagles hadn't made the postseason.

"And the Monday night win in '92 against Dallas was huge, too. We took it to the Cowboys on a Monday night game at the Vet—beat them 31-7 in front of a national audience. We just got the rhythm going that night and everything worked for us. And our defense! I really believe that Eagles D was as good a defense as ever played. At their height, they were as good as Pittsburgh's old Steel Curtain in the '70s. Despite the loss of Jerome Brown, the defense was still aggressive and intimidating. Mike Golic came in for Jerome and did a great job. And the D played fiercely against Dallas that Monday night.

"Then there was our playoff win over New Orleans. That was big, too. You know, after just spending all that time reviewing the Dallas game, how about if I switch gears? I'll go with our win over New Orleans. That's my pick—and it's really tough to pick—as the game of my life in Philadelphia."

Brian Baldinger was undrafted when he graduated from Duke University in 1982. He made the Dallas Cowboys and spent the next five years in Dallas before moving to Indianapolis, where he was named the Colts' Most Valuable Lineman in 1991. In '92, he blasted into Philly and spent two seasons as a Bird. Brian's fiery play contributed to the team's success in those transition years of the early '90s.

HOW WELL DO YOU KNOW YOUR BIRDS?

Brian Baldinger co-authored a book with Joy Van Skiver and Nadine Fischer a few years ago. What is the title of the book?

a) *Plain Talk from the NFL Trenches*
b) *A Map to Clear Messages: Conversations with a Wizard and a Warrior*
c) *How Battles Are Won and Lost*
d) *Sundays with Randall*
e) *Business Lessons from My Former Sunday Afternoons*
f) *Teaching the Fairer Sex the Finer Points of Football*
g) *My Career—From the Pits to the Booth*

MEET BRIAN BALDINGER

Born January 7, 1960, in Pittsburgh, Pennsylvania, Brian David Baldinger attended Massapequa High School in Long Island, New York. After graduation, he matriculated at Nassau Community College. There, he earned an associate's degree while starring in sports. As an all-league selection in football and the school's basketball MVP, Brian copped Nassau's Student Athlete of the Year Award. He transferred to Duke and was converted from tight end to offensive lineman.

After college, the Cowboys offered the undrafted Dukester a free agent contract. Of 107 rookies, Brian was the lone hopeful to earn a roster slot. The 6-foot-4, 278-pounder matured into a stalwart on the Cowboys' front line for five seasons before being dealt to Indianapolis. After a successful three-year stint with the Colts, he came to Philadelphia, arriving in the heyday of Philly's Buddy Ryan-crafted Gang Green Defense. After two seasons as an Eagles starter, No. 62 retired.

A few years later, he launched an active sports media career after completing studies at the Craig James School of Broadcasting (yes, the same Craig James who once was part of SMU's Pony Express backfield with Eric Dickerson and later a member of the Patriots). Brian has been a busy guy ever since. Call his cell phone and a booming voice invites the caller to leave a message for "Travel Dog." Travel Dog? "Yeah," chuckles the ex-lineman. "I got to calling myself Travel Dog because of all the globetrotting I did when I was working for NFL Europe. I've really been getting around these past several years. I've made it to six of the seven continents, so I've logged thousands of miles. I even got the opportunity to go on tour with Billy Joel and Bruce Springsteen.

"NFL Europe was what started me out traveling," Brian confides. "I started my broadcasting career doing color commentary on NFL Europe League games for Fox in 1997. The following season I joined the NFL on Fox, where I teamed with Ray Bentley and Curt Menefee. Curt and I partnered exclusively from '99 to 2001. Then I joined Joe Buck till 2002, when I worked with Pat Summerall."

Currently living in Marlton, New Jersey, Brian also hosts *Sports Talk* on New Jersey's CN8. Last year, he began co-hosting a One on One Sports national radio show.

THE BUILD-UP

After a 4-0 start to the 1992 season, the Birds slid into a big chill. The best they could manage was a lone win against the Cardinals while dropping contests to KC, Washington, and Green Bay. Right after Thanksgiving, they dropped a game to the 49ers, but then they caught fire. The Birds rattled off five straight victories to close out their second season under coach Rich Kotite. When they took the field against the New Orleans Saints, they were a smoking team that had shown a worrisome propensity for running hot and cold.

THE GAME OF MY LIFE
JANUARY 3, 1993

Brian Baldinger: "I tell you, this game was like two different games in one. In the first half, Jim Mora blitzed us and really had our offense confused. Then for some reason—I've always wanted to ask him why—he called off the dogs in the second half. We started to run the ball with success and Randall [Cunningham] made some big plays, and that was it. We got back into the game, turned the momentum around, and the entire complexion of the game changed.

"But in the first half, the Saints really stopped us. They had that awesome group of linebackers. [Yes, the '92 Saints did have great linebackers! Rickey Jackson, Vaughan Johnson, Sam Mills, and Pat Swilling—LBs all—made the Pro Bowl that year as the Saints led the league in QB sacks.] Randall made some heroic individual plays and the defense got us a safety and, well, it was a great ride back to Philly, too, after that win. It was always a nice ride back to Philly after a win.

"As for the game itself, we played in the Superdome in front of a huge crowd. We just couldn't get anything going for three quarters offensively. The Saints scored first on a short plunge by their big running back [that would be Craig "Ironhead" Heyward]. We came back on a long passing play [a 57-yarder, Cunningham to Barnett for six]. But then the Saints surged out and built up a pretty fair lead by halftime. [It was 17-7, Saints at the half: Morten Andersen had kicked a 35-yard three-pointer and Quinn Early, a Saints wide receiver, caught a 7-yard TD for their other scores.]

"I remember in the third quarter, we played kind of even. [Brian is correct: the two teams exchanged field goals to up the score to 20-10, New Orleans, going into the final quarter.] But then that's when the 'second game' … broke out.

"As I said, Randall started to make some heroic plays. He heaved one downfield to Fred Barnett again. It went for a score [a 35-yard TD]. I gotta say, those two, Randall Cunningham and Fred Barnett, were an underrated combo. Fred could go up and get the ball with the best of them, and when Randall was on his game, he could deliver the ball with the best of them. Put them together on a good day and they couldn't be stopped. Anyway, on the next play from scrimmage, as I recall, Seth Joyner picked one off and we went in for a score. I could feel things shift—the momentum and the passion. Yeah, the passion got big. We started running the ball well. Offensive linemen love to run the ball! And we scored on a [6-yard] run from Heath Sherman. That put us ahead for the first time. When New Orleans got the ball back, Reggie [White] sacked their QB [Bobby Hebert] in the end zone for a safety, and you could just feel it all slip away for the Saints. The whole stadium could feel it. That was all she wrote. It was our game."

WRAP

Indeed it was. Roger Ruzek tacked on a 39-yard field goal, and less than 20 seconds later, Eric Allen slammed the door shut on the Saints by picking off an errant Hebert throw and waltzing in for the final TD.

"HOW WELL DO YOU KNOW YOUR BIRDS?" ANSWER
b) *A Map to Clear Messages: Conversations with a Wizard and a Warrior*

Chapter 28

WILLIAM THOMAS

"SO, WHAT WAS THE GAME OF YOUR LIFE?"

(First conversation) William Thomas: "I've got to think about that one! Wow! I can think of so many games—so many big games—right now. I never stopped to think about the one game that I would call the game of my life, but now that you ask, I will. Let me think on this for a few days, and we'll talk about it then."

(Second conversation) William Thomas: "OK, tough choice, but here's the one I'm going with. It was the game against the Giants in 1995 when Ray Rhodes was coach. I had a couple of interceptions that game, and they helped win that game. We played a great defensive game all around that day—the whole unit. Winning the game set the stage for what I'd say was a good season, a surprise season. At least, I think we surprised some of our fans. So I'm going with that day as the game of my life—our win against the Giants in Giants Stadium."

William Thomas distinguished himself with his impressive athleticism. Packaging speed with agility and strength, William became a playmaker extraordinaire—a guy forever at the ready to turn a game around with an interception, fumble return, or sack. William was a favorite with the fans, who responded to the two-time Pro Bowler's make-something-happen aggressiveness on the field and his quiet, unassuming mien off it.

199

HOW WELL DO YOU KNOW YOUR BIRDS?

The Eagles have sent several guys to the Pro Bowl over the years. Some of them shared the same surname. Of the names on the list below, what is the only surname that was *not* shared by at least two Eagles Pro Bowlers? (For extra credit, what are the first names of each of the listed ex-Eagles Pro Bowlers?)

a) Barnes
c) Allen
e) Brown
b) Young
d) Thomas
f) Jackson

MEET WILLIAM THOMAS

Born August 13, 1968, William Harrison Thomas, Jr. attended Palo Duro (Spanish for "Hard Stick") High School before heading off to College Park, Texas, to don the maroon and white of Texas A & M University. Although William was a quarterback in high school, he was converted to defensive back his first couple of years in college. In his junior year, he switched to linebacker for good. These days, William confesses to having harbored a secret ambition to play tight end. "I had some talks with Jon Gruden about me playing tight end for the Eagles," William grins, "but we never really pursued the idea too seriously."

William Thomas boasted a stellar college career. The Texas A & M Aggies were ranked No. 15 nationally under head coach R.C. Slocum when William was a senior. Along with six of his teammates, William was selected in the NFL draft. Robert Wilson was the first Aggie chosen. The Buccaneers tapped the bruising 250-pound running back in the third round. In the next round, the Philadelphia Eagles selected William Thomas. Thomas was the 104th player picked in the draft. The young Texas native made the grade, as did fellow Eagles draftees Antone Davis, Rob Selby, and Andy Harmon. The Eagles rookie crop that season was outstanding. As for William Thomas, the 6-foot-2, 223-pound linebacker immediately contributed by notching up the athleticism of the

---

Linebacker William Thomas runs the ball in a 17-14 victory over the New York Giants on October 15, 1995. *Bill Hickey/Getty Images*

Birds' already outstanding linebacker corps. At that time, the 'backer corps was anchored by Byron Evans and Seth Joyner.

William joined Philadelphia as the dynasty that Buddy Ryan had cobbled together was disintegrating. Buddy's charges never succeeded in making it to the top. In an interview I did at the time with blustery team owner Norman Braman in *Delaware Valley* magazine prior to Buddy's last year, Braman guaranteed not only a Super Bowl appearance but a Super Bowl victory. When his fatuous ambition crashed and burned, Braman didn't renew his irascible coach's contract. Thus, William's first mentor turned out to be Rich Kotite, Coach Buddy's offensive coordinator, who became the franchise's 18th head coach. Kotite ended up piloting the Birds to a 10-6 record. Though the mark equaled that of his predecessor the previous season, the '91 squad failed to secure a playoff berth.

As for William Thomas' rookie season, he made seven starts. For the most part, he shared right linebacker duties with Jessie Small. (William made seven starts, Jessie eight.) Despite being a part-timer, William ranked sixth on the team in sacks and 10th in tackles—impressive numbers, considering the caliber of that Eagles defense. The Birds were such a defensive juggernaut that all five members of the '91 Eagles Pro Bowl contingent were defenders: Eric Allen, Jerome Brown, Seth Joyner, Clyde Simmons, and Reggie White. The following year, William laid sole claim to the right linebacker position and chipped in with 94 tackles.

Unfortunately, William's rapid personal ascendancy in the ensuing years coincided with a lackluster period in Eagles history. The Birds were sliding into the NFL abyss under Kotite, leveling off to 8-8 in 1993 before dipping below .500 in '94. Nonetheless, William Thomas was establishing a reputation as one of the league's solid performers during that skid. His sack totals in '93 and '94 were 6.5 and six, respectively.

Meanwhile, more winds of change were blowing in Philly. In May of 1994, Jeffrey Lurie bought the Philadelphia franchise from Norman Braman. The '94 season turned out as strange as any in the memory of many Philadelphians—and Philadelphia teams have authored more than their fair share of bizarre seasons. The '94 Eagles kicked off the season in Super Bowl fashion. Though they lost the opener, a 28-23 affair at New York, they followed with seven successive wins. At that point, they came completely undone, failing to win a single game the rest of the way. For the first time since 1982, the Eagles didn't place a single representative on the All-Pro team.

The collapse spelled the end of Rich Kotite. In 1995, under new head coach Ray Rhodes, the Eagles rebounded and made the playoffs. By 1996, William Thomas had established his reputation as one of the league's premier playmaking linebackers and was selected for the Pro Bowl three consecutive seasons. Number 51 was voted Eagles Defensive MVP three consecutive years (1995-1997).

William continued to excel as an Eagle through 1999. He then closed out his career with two seasons in Oakland. When William called it quits in 2002, he had played in 172 games, registering 37 sacks, picking off 27 interceptions, and scoring 26 points, all on defense.

Today, William lives not far from the Philadelphia area in Mullica Hill, New Jersey, with his wife, Susan, and three boys. William sells real estate when he's not hauling his active sons around on their supercharged sport schedules.

BUILDING UP TO THE GAME

The '95 season was in its seventh week. The Eagles headed up the Jersey Turnpike to the always hostile confines of Giant Stadium to write another chapter in this traditionally fierce inter-conference rivalry. Both the Eagles and the Giants were off to disappointing starts. At 3-3, the Eagles had already succumbed to three non-divisional opponents: Tampa Bay, San Diego, and Oakland. That was the bad news. The good news was that they registered Ws against two divisional opponents: the hapless Arizona Cardinals and the Washington Redskins. To whip Washington, they had to go into overtime. The Birds were coming off that OT win when they faced New York. The Giants entered the game at 2-4. They were desperate to turn their season around because 5-1 Dallas was running away with the East.

Ray Rhodes was in his rookie season as Philadelphia's head coach. As always in Philadelphia, expectations were high. Thus, when Rhodes' team opened the campaign in front of the Philly throng with a flat 21-6 loss to Tampa Bay, the hometown fans were not happy. Midway through the season, they remained unhappy.

Randall Cunningham started the season at quarterback. However, after four sub-par performances, Rodney Peete replaced him. The Birds lost three of the first four games with Randall as starter. With Peete inserted into the lineup, the Eagles squeaked to a far-from-convincing

15-10 win over the Saints. With Rodney again at the helm the following week, the Eagles lit Washington up with 37 points. Thus, the Birds squared off against the Giants on October 15, riding an unconvincing two-game win streak.

The Giants were suffering their own headaches. Dallas and New York were the one-two finishers in the Eastern Division in '94. Thus far in 1995, New York was muddling and mucking around like a rudderless ship. At least, that's what the New York papers were portraying before the game. In the Big Apple, the battle with the Birds was heralded as a must-win for the Giants—the game that would free the Giants from their mediocre funk. So 74,252 screaming Giants fans (excuse the redundancy) assaulted the Meadowlands on October 15, 1995, to celebrate a Giants triumph.

THE GAME OF MY LIFE
OCTOBER 15, 1995

William Thomas: "I think you tend to remember games by how your unit performed. What I mean is, the offense did not have a good day against the Giants, but the defense, well, it was one of our finest days. I had a memorable performance because of the two interceptions I came up with, but I wasn't the only guy who turned in a fine performance. Mike Zordich had a day to remember, too. He ran a fumble back for a score, and then, as the game was winding down, came up with a big pick that sealed the win. So I remember this game because it did turn our season around. We were only 3-3 up to that point and ended up making the playoffs.

"We started off slow that day. Actually, both teams did, as I recall. [That's correct: the first quarter ended with double goose eggs on the scoreboard.] I remember the weather wasn't ideal for the passing game, either. Giant Stadium can be tough on quarterbacks with the wind, and that day there were plenty of pretty big gusts. But we basically stopped not only the passing game, but the running game as well. I've got to call it a joint success—the coaching staff and my defensive teammates. What happened was that we fooled the Giants offense. The coaching staff came up with the strategy and then the defense executed it well. Dave Brown, the Giants' QB, was a solid quarterback, but our coaches felt that we could confuse him with different looks on defense. We tried to disguise the coverage so he thought he was looking at man coverage when it was actually zone coverage and vice versa.

"In the second quarter, our offense got a nice drive going. I remember we marched down the field mostly on runs, and then Ricky Watters carried it in for a score on a beautiful run. The offensive line executed real well on that drive. [The Eagles went 80 yards in 10 plays. The big plays were runs of 13 and 14 yards by Watters and a 29-yard Peete to Charlie Garner pass.] Then the defense got a score. That big Giants running back, Rodney Hampton, fumbled, and Mike Zordich scooped it up and took it to the house [for a 58-yard TD]. We stopped Hampton and the Giants' running game all day long. [The Giants gained only 84 yards on 23 carries, while Hampton was held to 58 yards on 14 carries.]

"Anyway, the Giants, I think, only had a field goal in the first half. [Actually, William's memory is one field goal shy—NY kicker Brad Daluiso nailed two three-pointers in the first half.] In the second half, Randall came in at quarterback to replace Rodney Peete, who got a concussion in the first half. The Giants replaced their quarterback in the second half, too. Dave Brown went out and Tommy Maddox replaced him. I think the Giants were kind of stalled, and the coach [Dan Reeves] was looking to get somebody in there who could get the offense moving. They obviously tried to make some adjustments to their offensive game plan in the second half. They started running more curl routes and down and outs against what they thought was a zone defense. Anyway, in the third quarter, I had dropped back into the secondary on this particular play. I read Maddox from the start—read his eyes. I could see from the snap where he was going with the pass, so I stepped in front of Aaron Pierce and picked it off. I loved to drop back into the secondary on pass defense. I think that was one of my strengths. Anyway, I got lucky again a few possessions later and intercepted another pass from Maddox.

"We had the Giants down 17-6 late in the fourth quarter and it looked like it was our game to keep. Our offense still wasn't moving. They never really got it going all day, but our defense had NY stopped. Then the Giants came up with a big play. Our punter fumbled the snap and they blocked the punt. [Tom Hutton was the Eagles punter—not the Phillies' now-retired, average-hitting Tom Hutton who inscrutably morphed into Rogers Hornsby whenever he faced Tom Seaver.] Somebody picked it up and ran it back for a score. [New York's Keith

Elias blocked the punt and his teammate, Omar Douglas, ran it in.] Then the Giants went for two points and Rodney Hampton delivered. All of a sudden, it's a 17-14 game.

"Our offense still couldn't move and the Giants got the ball back. There was less than a minute left and the Giants were about 15 yards away from trying a field goal, and that's when Zordich got the INT. We ran the clock out and won 17-14.

"That win seemed to set the team off. ... I'll always remember that game. I contributed two interceptions and had the pleasure of playing with a great defensive unit in a key game that eventually led us to the playoffs. You never forget days like that."

WRAP

As William Thomas proudly notes, the win over the Giants effectively knocked the Giants out of the playoff chase. It was the Eagles' third win that season over division opponents, giving the Birds the advantage in a wild-card showdown. They succeeded and made the playoffs. In the first round, they spanked Detroit 58-37 in another unforgettable Philly-high game. That game, too, was memorable for William Thomas. He returned an interception 37 yards for a TD to seal the Eagles victory.

In an interesting epilogue to his Philly career, William landed with the Oakland Raiders. He and another former Eagles legend, Eric Allen, happened to close out their careers in one of the NFL's most storied and controversial contests. Both men were on the field when the New England Patriots beat the Raiders in the January 19, 2002, divisional playoff game. That was the game in which QB Tom Brady attempted a pass in the waning minutes and had the ball knocked out of his grasp. Originally ruled a fumble, the call was reversed by referee Walt Coleman. The ref based his decision on the "tuck rule." The Pats retained possession and went on to win not only the game, but the Super Bowl. In fact, New England rolled off three Super Bowl victories, the third—as Philadelphians remember painfully—at the expense of the Eagles.

"HOW WELL DO YOU KNOW YOUR BIRDS?" ANSWER

c) Allen (Eric Allen is the only "Allen" who ever represented the Eagles in the Pro Bowl.)

EXTRA CREDIT:

a) Barnes: Walt and Billy Ray
b) Young: Charles and Roynell
d) Thomas: William and William (formerly Tra)
e) Brown: Tim, Bob, and Jerome
f) Jackson: Harold and Keith

Chapter 29

DAVE SPADARO

"SO, WHAT WAS THE GAME OF YOUR LIFE?"

Dave Spadaro: "They all are—every game. I love this organization. I love being here and doing all the things I do for the organization. So really, I enjoy every minute of every game. But if I have to pick out one particular game—one memorable game—it has to be the NFC championship game. We finally got past the hurdle we couldn't get past the three previous years. And, of course, getting past that hurdle got us to the Super Bowl. That's the purpose for the whole season. So I look back at those three preceding tries, and, well, it just sweetens the memories of that game in 2005.

"The first year [January 27, 2002] against the Rams, we were considered as, sort of, the upstart Eagles. And we came oh-so-close to topping the Rams. It hurt to lose, but then again, we had come so far just to get there in the first place. Then the following year, we lost a bitter game to Tampa Bay. That loss was very tough to take. We went into the game with such hope, but I think the following season it hurt even more to lose. The week before, we had just managed to squeak by Green Bay in overtime. Then we played Carolina in the NFC championship game. It was the last game ever played at the Vet, so we wanted this game—this memory—to be something special or historic. It didn't turn out that way, unfortunately. We lost to Carolina in a game where it seemed we simply never could get started. Those three consecutive losses made the win in

2005 all the more sweet. We knew we were ready and we went into that game with the kind of confidence that good teams—mature teams—have. And it all worked out. What a day!"

To Iggles fans, Dave Spadaro is one of the more recognizable faces in the Philadelphia Eagles organization. Dave, or "Spuds," does the sideline reporting on all Eagles preseason games. He's also the front man for all the team's publications, the motive force and behind the Eagles' tremendously award-winning website, and a frequent personality on radio and TV.

HOW WELL DO YOU KNOW YOUR BIRDS?

Since the Eagles first appeared in a postseason game (December 21, 1947, when they beat the Pittsburgh Steelers 21-0 for the Eastern Division championship), what has been their longest dry spell between postseason playoff appearances?

a) 5 years

b) 8 years

c) 12 years

d) 15 years

e) 18 years

f) 22 years

MEET DAVE SPADARO

Dave Spadaro graduated from West Chester's Henderson High School in 1983 before attending Temple University. As a frosh Owl, he, like the Voice of the Eagles, Merrill Reese, worked on the school's radio station, WRTI. As an upperclassman, Dave assumed the role of play-by-play man for the Temple men's basketball team. Dave earned his bachelor of arts degree in radio, television, and film in 1987. By then, he was a full-time employee at the *Daily Local News* in West Chester, Pennsylvania. That year, his column on then-Eagles tight end Keith Jackson garnered first-place honors in the Keystone State Journalism Awards.

In 1989, he became the editor of *Eagles Digest* and has been covering the Eagles on an everyday basis ever since. In 1997, Dave became part of the Eagles organization as director of publications. A year later, Dave took over the team's website on the Internets (as it is known in the Oval Office). He retains those responsibilities to this day.

PhiladelphiaEagles.com has been recognized as the best website in the NFL the last three years, winning five awards all-told in league voting. The site was also named the league's best website by *The Sports Business Journal* in 2005.

Dave, now 41, is married to Lori. The couple has two children, Danny (11) and Julia (9), and the family resides in suburban Philadelphia.

BUILDING UP TO THE GAME

"There was a snowstorm the night before," Dave Spadaro recalls. "My wife and I were in Havertown on the eve of the game. The snow made the whole scene really festive, and for some reason, it just gave an air that things seemed right, like this was some sort of sign that it would finally be our time—our year. The Eagles were confident—I'd say quietly confident. We needed a great defensive plan to contain Michael Vick, the Atlanta quarterback. We were confident that Jim Johnson, our defensive coordinator, would come up with one.

"We set a club record that year for most pass completions [336] and most yards gained [4,208] in a season. We had acquired Terrell Owens and our passing attack was topnotch. We went 13-3. ... "

In four of the first six games, the Birds eclipsed the 30-point mark. In game five, they destroyed Carolina 30-8 at the Linc to avenge their January 18, 2004, NFC championship game loss to those same Panthers. In game eight, after having cruised through the first half of the season virtually unchallenged, the Eagles suffered a comeuppance in the form of a 27-3 setback against the Steelers at Heinz Field. Undaunted, the Birds picked themselves up, dusted themselves off, and started all over again with a five-game win streak bookended with wins over Dallas. The first win over Dallas was a Monday night national showcase in which the Birds scored 49. In thumping the 'Boys, the Eagles equaled a couple all-time franchise bests. Their 35 first-half points matched their effort on October 23, 1949, against Washington. Their 18 second-quarter points equaled their previous best output on November 19, 1967, versus the Giants. Lito Sheppard also returned an interception for the longest return in Eagles history—a 101-yard romp after he picked off Vinny Testaverde. The final win of the five-game streak was a tight 12-7 squeaker in which Terrell Owens went down with an ankle injury.

Fortunately, the Eagles had clinched their division already. They closed out the season with two losses as fans and pundits alike pondered if the loss of Owens would cripple the offense and crush Super Bowl hopes. However, the resilient hometowners trounced the Minnesota Vikings 27-14 sans Owens at Lincoln Financial Field in the NFC divisional playoff game that set up the NFC championship game, where they again took the field without their problematic wide receiver.

THE GAME OF MY LIFE
JANUARY 23, 2005

Dave Spadaro: "It was frigid that day, that's for sure, but the atmosphere was amazing. I don't think anyone in the stands sat down the whole day. Nobody noticed the cold. I think it was about a foot of snow officially that fell the day before. …

"We played superbly all over the field and notably from right end to left end. Derrick Burgess on the right and Jevon Kearse contained Michael Vick all day. [Vick was held that day to 162 yards: 136 passing, 26 running.] The whole defense was hitting everything that moved—punishing hits. Hollis Thomas laid a huge lick on Vick and Brian Dawkins rocked Algie Crumpler [Atlanta's All-Pro tight end] so you could feel the ground shake.

"On offense, the Eagles were efficient. I think everyone close to the Eagles was proud and happy for Chad Lewis when he scored those two touchdowns. Those catches were things of beauty, both of them, but it was the fact that Chad had been in Philly so long and was such a hard worker and he was hurting that day, so those two TD catches were special. Anyway, his performance fit right into the theme of the day. His wife came down to the field after the game, and Chad was wearing Leo Carlin's shirt. Then I have this vision: Todd Pinckston and Fred Mitchell running around with Freddie's People's Champ Belt. Do you remember that belt Freddie had? I have no idea why that sticks out. I guess the whole scene was surreal. The whole city went wild. I think that's the loudest I ever heard the Linc. You know, I've never even looked back at the tape of that game. It's all fixed in my memory. Sometimes it seems like it happened just yesterday. Other times, it seems like it was a zillion years ago. Anyway, that NFL championship game was the greatest day—the game I remember most.

WRAP

The Eagles took an early 7-0 lead when Dorsey Levens lugged one in from 4 yards out. In the second quarter, Atlanta engineered a 64-yard drive. The drive stalled when, with first and goal at the Eagles' 2-yard line, Hollis Thomas made a bone-jarring hit on Michael Vick. The Falcons had to be content with a 23-yard field goal.

The Eagles answered with a TD. The key play of the drive was a Donovan McNabb completion to Fred Mitchell on a third-and-11. On the next play, he followed with a 45-yard toss to Greg Lewis. Two plays later, McNabb found Chad Lewis for the first of Lewis' two scoring nabs.

The Falcons bounced right back with a 10-yard scoring romp by Warrick Dunn, which narrowed the gap to 14-10 at halftime. However, that was all she wrote for the Falcons. They were shut out thereafter. The Birds drove 60 yards with the second-half kickoff as David Akers tacked on a three-pointer from 31 yards out. Aikens added another 34-yard three-pointer before the third quarter ended. In the fourth quarter, McNabb and Lewis hooked up again for a TD as the Eagles sealed their trip to Super Bowl XXXIX.

"HOW WELL DO YOU KNOW YOUR BIRDS?" ANSWER
e) 18 years (The Eagles did not appear in a postseason game from December 26, 1960, until December 24, 1978—I'm ignoring, of course, the travesty known as the Runner-up Bowl, an ill-fated spectacle that died of ennui a few years after its 1961 debut.

Chapter 30

BRIAN DAWKINS

"SO, WHAT WAS THE GAME OF YOUR LIFE?"

Brian Dawkins: "It has to be the 2004 NFC championship game. We fought to get there for a few years, and it all came together for us that game. After we failed three consecutive years in that game, there was a lot of 'here we go again' sentiment around the city. We overcame that. We overcame everything and won a big game convincingly. I don't think I ever got as much satisfaction as I did from that game."

Brian Dawkins boasts tenure among the current crop of Birds. He has been rocking opponents' worlds to the oohs and ahs of the partisan Philly crowd since 1996. The Eagles' "old man" is still doing his thing with no sign of abatement. Along with Shawn Andrews, "Dawk" was the only Eagle honored as an All Pro in 2006. He was also named the 2006 Pro Bowl starter at strong safety. Of course, Brian Dawkins is no stranger to the Pro Bowl squad. At this time, he's a six-time repeat defender. In addition, he was named the first alternate in 2000.

Brian finished the 2006 season ranked third on the Eagles' all-time interception list. Brian's future Hall of Fame pedigree rests on a number of laurels. For one, No. 20 ranks sixth on the NFL's all-time list for most career sacks by a defensive back. He is also one of only eight NFL players ever to record at least 25 INTs and 15 sacks. (Apologies to pre-1982 players: sack stats were not kept till after 1982.) The Clemson product is durable and

215

tough. He currently ranks third, right behind Harold Carmichael and Chuck Bednarik, on the Eagles' all-time list for most games played.

HOW WELL DO YOU KNOW YOUR BIRDS?

Bill Bradley and Eric Allen are tied for the Eagles all-time lead in interceptions with 34. Which of these defensive backs listed below has more career interceptions as an Eagle than Brian Dawkins?

a) Ernie Steele

b) Tom Brookshier

c) Jerry Norton

d) Herm Edwards

e) Joe Scarpati

f) Troy Vincent

g) Bobby Taylor

h) Don Burroughs

MEET BRIAN DAWKINS

Brian Patrick Dawkins, Sr. is the guy who transforms on game day from quiet, mild-mannered Brian into … well, Wolverine. Wolverine? Yes, Wolverine, as in Hugh Jackman's X-Men character. Wolverine is known for his keen animal senses and instinct. That's the connection. Wolverine action figures monopolize the top shelf of Brian Dawkins' Eagles locker. Mirroring Wolverine's modus operandi, Brian transforms the moment he hits the gridiron. Opponents won't take issue with that assertion. Neither will football analysts. *The Sporting News* chose him as the hardest hitter in the NFL in 2004. He's a ball hawk, too. Dawkins currently has more interceptions as an Eagle than any other NFL player has for his respective team.

Born October 13, 1973, Brian started blazing a trail of gridiron excellence as a high schooler. He earned All-State honors at Raines High School in Jacksonville, Florida, where he helped lead his team to 30 straight victories. His high school alma mater inducted him into its Hall of Fame, which reads like a who's who in the NFL. The Eagles have struck gold at Raines High on a few occasions. Among Raines' alumni are all-time leading Eagles receiver Harold Carmichael, current star Lito

---

Brian Dawkins has played with the Philadelphia Eagles for over 10 years. *AP Images*

Sheppard, and Jabar Gaffney. (Packers WR Rod Gardner is another contemporary NFL employee.) Like Carmichael, Brian Dawkins also earned all-conference honors in basketball at Raines.

Dawk moved on to Clemson University to play college football. He was a three-year starter for the Tigers. In his senior year, the 6-foot tall athlete was elected all-conference as he led the Atlantic Coast Conference in interceptions with six. He was named the first-team strong safety on Clemson's all-centennial team in 1995.

Brian was an Eagles second-round draft choice who broke into the starting lineup right away. His career has spanned one of the most extended periods of excellence in Eagles history. (The Birds have made the playoffs every year from 2000 to 2006, with the exception of 2005, the year of the cleanup following the train wreck that was Terrell Owens.) Therefore, it's no surprise that Brian holds the Eagles' all-time record for most playoff games (15). He boasts multiple team and league honors. Dawk has won the Eagles Defensive MVP Award three times (1999, 2002, and 2004). He was named Defensive Player of the Week for the week of September 29, 2002. In December 2006, he was named Defensive Player of the Month. He has also distinguished himself in Pro Bowl appearances. His two interceptions in the 2000 Pro Bowl tie for the record for most NFC interceptions in the spectacle.

Over the course of his NFL career, Brian has built himself up from 190 pounds to a rock-solid 210. He credits dedication to a demanding training regimen. He used to train in the off-season with ultimate fighting champion Tim "Obake" Catalfo. When Catalfo moved, former teammate Levon Kirkland hipped Brian to another trainer, Jeff Higuera. Brian feels that Higuera has improved both his flexibility and strength. Higuera's theory focuses on working two muscle groups simultaneously. The goal is to improve stability and balance. In concert with the Higuera workout, Brian follows a supplementary program designed to reduce injuries and quicken recovery.

BUILDING UP TO THE GAME

"We had strong teams from the 2000 season on," Brian Dawkins explains. "We just never quite managed to get over the top. As far as I was concerned, we failed. Our goal was always winning a Super Bowl, and as good as we were and as good as we felt we were, we didn't achieve that objective. We should have won those big games those first few years, but we didn't.

"But in 2004, our team was so strong. We were so confident that year. Every game that year, every time we took the field, we never even considered losing. The only question as far as we were concerned was not whether we'd win, but how much we'd win by. When we got to the NFC championship game against Atlanta in 2004, we were determined we weren't going to lose. Like I said, we had been to that point four straight times and came up short. This time we felt we could not fail."

THE GAME OF MY LIFE
JANUARY 23, 2005

Brian Dawkins: "It was a cold day. [Yes it was! It was 17 degrees at the kickoff with winds from the northwest gusting from 26 to 35 miles an hour. The wind chill was below zero and a foot of snow had fallen across much of the region the evening before.] I don't think the weather bothered a guy on our squad. The only thing we were focused on was winning. We went into the game determined to prove the doubters wrong. The so-called experts were claiming that our defense couldn't stop Atlanta's running game. That year, Atlanta was the top running team in football. None of that noise bothered us. I'd say it made us stronger because we felt slighted. But the way the weather turned out—where it was not only cold, but windy—supposedly favored Atlanta even more. We were the team that relied on the pass more, and the wind gusts were supposed to hurt our offense more than Atlanta's. Like I said, none of that talk mattered. Our defense went out there that day to get the ball to our offense as much as possible. We were out there to make big plays and we wanted to keep Atlanta's offense off the field as much as possible.

"I think our defense set the tone on the first series of plays. We shut them right down. Michael Vick, their quarterback, never got started and never got untracked. [Vick carried the ball 11 times, but gained only 24 yards and often threw wildly in the wind, completing only 11 of 24 attempts.] Then, in the second quarter, Hollis Thomas made a big play. Atlanta was set to score, or that's what they thought. I think we were up by a TD, and they were on our 3-yard line. Hollis broke through and sacked Vick. They kicked a field goal and we never looked back.

"I made a couple big hits myself that game—one on Michael Vick, the other on their tight end, Alge Crumpler. We were hitting the Falcons all over the field all day long. We never stopped. That's why I was so emotional at the end of the game. I remember holding that championship trophy over my head and talking to the crowd over the public-address system, saying, 'Nobody respected us as a defense. Give me some respect right now.'

"The fans were great that day. They were as excited as we were. So that game, that's the game of my life. I had an interception, too, off Michael Vick. I felt good the whole game. I felt confident, and we played the kind of football we were capable of in front of the home crowd. It was a great day."

WRAP

Unfortunately, the Eagles couldn't keep the magic rolling for one more game. They played the Patriots two weeks later at Alltel Stadium in Jacksonville, Florida. That was like coming home for Brian Dawkins. The Birds played well, almost well enough to win—but not quite. "It was our fault," Brian Dawkins contends. "We didn't make the plays when it mattered. New England did. That's what happened."

It was a tough, exciting, evenly matched game—the only Super Bowl in history in which the two combatants were knotted at the end of the third quarter. The Eagles outgained the Pats 369-331, but that advantage went for naught when, with less than a minute remaining, New England DB Rodney Harrison picked off his second McNabb pass of the day and doused the Eagles' dream.

"HOW WELL DO YOU KNOW YOUR BIRDS?" ANSWER
d) Herm Edwards (Through 2006, Brian had 32 interceptions. Edwards had 33.)

Chapter 31

LITO SHEPPARD

"SO, WHAT WAS THE GAME OF YOUR LIFE?"

Lito Sheppard: "I think our first game against Dallas in 2006 is the game I remember most. I'll remember that game for a long time. There was so much hype about it! I was just coming back from an ankle injury—actually, two ankle injuries—and we were playing in front of the home crowd. Philly was more fired up about winning than I've ever seen. Really, everyone in the nation had their eyes on this game because of the whole TO [Terrell Owens] situation. I was fortunate to come up big in the game, so yeah, I'll always remember this one!"

It took but a short time for Lito Sheppard to get his motor up and running in Philadelphia after an outstanding college career at Florida. A first-round draft choice, he broke in with the Eagles in 2002, when one of the Eagles' all-time great CB tandems—Bobby Taylor and Troy Vincent—was at its peak. Lito still managed to see action in a dozen contests as a rookie. The following year, he made his first start against New England in the second game of the season. As a soph, No. 26 wound up starting nine games. In 2004, he was promoted to a full-fledged starter. Since assuming that role, Lito has picked off more enemy passes than any of his compadres. He turned in a stellar 2006 season and appears destined for greatness.

HOW WELL DO YOU KNOW YOUR BIRDS?

Which Eagles quarterback holds the NFL record for most consecutive completions?

a) Davey O'Brien   b) Randall Cunningham
c) Ron Jaworski   d) Norm Van Brocklin
e) King Hill   f) Sonny Jurgensen
g) Donovan McNabb   h) Tommy Thompson
i) Bobby Thomason   j) Roman Gabriel
k) Norm Snead

MEET LITO SHEPPARD

Born April 8, 1981, in Jacksonville, Florida, Lito Decorian Sheppard is another Raines High product (along with Harold Carmichael, Brian Dawkins, and Jabar Gaffney) that the Eagles coaxed north. He established himself as a blue-chip prospect as a high schooler. In fact, in his senior year at Raines in 1998, he was named the top defensive back in the nation by *Bluechips*. He was also voted Jacksonville's Defensive Player of the Year.

Lito's collegiate career at Florida was no less impressive. In three seasons as a starter, Lito was a two-time All-American. He ranks fourth in total yards on punt returns on the Gators' illustrious list of punt returners, behind Jacquez Green, Ivory Curry, and Ricky Nattiel. He also distinguished himself as only the fourth Gator to be selected an All-American as a sophomore.

As an Eagle, Lito has filled the starting CB slot marvelously. In his first complete season as a starter, the 5-foot-10, 194-pound competitor returned an interception 101 yards, which, as it turns out, merely penciled his name in the franchise's all-time record book. Lito's sprint was the team's longest individual interception return ever—to that point. He pilfered five other opponents' passes that year and became the first Eagle since Eric Allen in 1993 (and only the fourth Eagle in history) to return two interceptions for TDs in a single season. His second TD that year came on a 64-yard INT of a Jake Delhomme pass. In that same game against Carolina, Lito picked another one off during the Panthers' final

Lito Sheppard snags a pass intended for Terrell Owens (No. 81) in the fourth quarter of a game played on Sunday, October 8, 2006. *AP Images*

drive. For his heroics that day, he received his first NFC Defensive Player of the Week Award.

In 2005, Lito was in the midst of another solid season. He was leading the team with three interceptions when he suffered a season-ending high ankle sprain in the third quarter of a Giants game. Lito came back in 2006 and responded with perhaps his finest year. He broke the mark he set two years prior when he scooted 102 yards to pay dirt with an interception.

Lito makes his home in Philly, at least part of the time. The rest of the time, he's in Florida. Lito married a Florida alumna, Nicole, at Disney World in the 2005 off-season. When he's relaxing off the gridiron, he's an avowed TV junkie who tunes in to *American Chopper*, *Fear Factor*, *Junkyard Wars*, and, inscrutably, *Jeopardy*.

BUILDING UP TO THE GAME

I was leaving Citizens Bank Park after a Phillies game in July. The parking lot was full of guys hawking T-shirts. Nothing unusual there, but the T-shirts they were pushing had nothing to do with the Phillies or an upcoming rock concert. On the front, the T-shirts read, "Dallas Sucks." On the back, they read—well, let's just say they said something about Terrell Owens and some follow-up action on his part. The T-shirts were selling like hotcakes. With the entire TO saga coloring all things Eagles, the Birds imploded and took a tumultuous tumble from their accustomed Andy Reid-era playoff berth. Demonstrating self-control, calmness, and reclaimed rationality, the front office, management, and players reconstructed and reconstituted. The 2006 edition came back and, late in the season, launched one of the more exciting playoff runs in recent history.

The Eagles started the season off like a house afire. By the time Dallas was coming to town in NFL week number five, the Birds were 3-1. They sat alone atop the Eastern Division, though 2-1 Dallas was barking at their heels. The Giants stood at 2-2, which set the Philly-Dallas match up as a clash for divisional supremacy.

This multidimensional match was pure Hollywood or, perhaps, pure WWF. The whole city had been waiting for this game—the game stadium parking-lot hawkers had been hyping since mid-summer. Terrell Owens' tiresome act had plummeted his popularity in Philly lower than the Joker's in Gotham City. To make matters worse, when Owens left town for what he perceived were greener pastures, he ended up cavorting on the grassy knoll of Texas Stadium for the Quaker City's most despised rival in any sport. The situation itself was Shakespearean, although Shakespeare probably wouldn't have written about it. He fancied depth in his characters.

As for Lito Sheppard, he felt some unspoken anguish about the match. "I was just coming back from an ankle injury," Lito recalls. "Actually, I was coming back from two ankle injuries. I had a season-ending ankle injury in 2005. Then I missed three games in 2006 when I injured the other ankle in the opener! So this was my first game back. Frankly, I was entering this game with two ankles that weren't 100 percent.

"This game was special in so many ways. Obviously, there was the whole TO thing, but the Eagles as a team had a lot to prove, too. We wanted to show everyone, especially our fans, that we were back and we were contenders. Then again, this was a division game, so it was all the more important. [It sure was—the Eagles needed to gain some respect. They had lost seven straight games to divisional opponents going into this matchup.] It was early in the season, but everyone on the team and everyone in the city considered this game a must-win. We had already lost a game we should never have lost to the Giants. That was the second game of the year. It was our worst game of the season—the toughest loss to take. We had the game in our hands and let it get away. [The Eagles had a 24-7 lead with 10:55 left in the third period and blew the game 30-24.]

"Personally, I was nervous. Yeah, I'm being honest. I was really nervous. I didn't know how to approach the game. I remember telling the trainers all that before the game. I mean, I was mentally and physically prepared, but I had concerns about my ankles and just the whole hype of the game."

If Lito was nervous, the Eagles need to find a way to make him more nervous every Sunday. He overcame any jitters he might have felt and turned in the game of his life.

THE GAME OF MY LIFE
OCTOBER 8, 2006

Lito Sheppard: "We were really ready for that game. Everybody was sky high, especially the fans [all 69,268 of them]! Our defense went out on the field to hit. Our pass rush was getting to Drew Bledsoe, the Dallas quarterback, time and again. [The Birds sacked Bledsoe seven times.] I don't know how many turnovers we caused. [The 'Boys fumbled four times—the Eagles caused two of them.] I had two interceptions. Brian Dawkins had one. We converted on a lot of those turnovers. [Philadelphia scored 17 points on turnovers.] The offense—and especially Donovan McNabb—was really hot. [Donovan was 18-33 for 354 yards and two TDs.]

"The offense had some pretty plays. Hank Baskett caught his first pro TD pass. He made a nice double move on their safety [Pat Watkins] and scored a long touchdown [an 87-yarder].

"Like I said, we were pumped. That excitement came out in me as a bit of nervousness, but it might have elevated my play! We got out fast with a couple of scores. [The Eagles jumped out 10-0 when Dallas punter Matt McBriar fumbled a snap on a punt and the Eagles converted it into seven. Bledsoe fumbled on the ensuing series and David Akers kicked a 27-yard field goal.]

"I think we fell behind after that quick start. [Dallas roared back to a 14-10 lead.] I almost came up with an interception in the second period. We had a good rush on Bledsoe on this play—as I said, we had a good rush on him all day—and somebody hit his arm. The ball fluttered out and I had it in my hands, but didn't hold on.

"I think it was the third quarter when Hank caught that long TD. We went out ahead again on his TD and never lost the lead.

"In the fourth quarter we were ahead, but Dallas was driving. They advanced the ball inside the 25-yard line on a third-down play. Bledsoe tried to hit TO with a pass. Fortunately, I stepped in and intercepted it. We didn't score and Dallas got the ball back. On a third-down play with a little over two minutes left, I stepped in and broke up a pass intended for Terry Glenn. Then Dallas went for it on fourth down and short yardage and kept the drive alive.

"After the two-minute warning it looked like we had them beat, but they got a pass-interference call [against Michael Lewis] and Dallas ended up with the ball on the 6-yard line. At the time, they were only down by a TD [31-24], so everyone in the stadium was on their feet. On second down, Bledsoe was looking for Jason Witten. We were in a coverage where Witten was my responsibility if he turned outside, but if he stayed inside, Jeremiah Trotter had to cover him. Jeremiah had him closed off inside, so Witten tried to break to the outside. I just happened to read what he was doing as it was happening and got in position.

"My mentality whenever I come up with an interception is to look for an opening and try to take it back all the way. I always figure if I can get by that first wave on the return, I can make it all the way. If I break clear, they can't catch me. That's what happened on this play. I didn't realize I had broken my own record till all the guys told me about it. [Lito returned the pick 102 yards for a new Eagles record that eclipsed the 101-yard standard he had set two years earlier.]

"What a game! With all the hype and with all my nervousness I felt going in, it all turned out great for the Eagles and me. And those Philly fans—we did not want to let them down. It was such a feeling of satisfaction to hear all that crowd noise after my score and to know that we had beaten Dallas!"

WRAP

A lot of Eagles came up big in the Dallas game. Darwin Walker had three sacks on the day. Donovan McNabb came up with big play after big play. When the stadium lights went out, the 4-1 Eagles were alone atop of the Eastern Division. The Cowboys and Giants each had two losses.

The Birds, unfortunately, doused the euphoria of the Dallas win with three straight losses in its wake. They managed a win against the hapless Washington Redskins, but their record slipped to 5-6 with only five games remaining. They appeared to be a team in freefall, going nowhere. Then, remarkably, they found new life and surged to 10-6 to claim another NFC championship.

"HOW WELL DO YOU KNOW YOUR BIRDS?" ANSWER

b) Randall Cunningham (He completed his last 10 passes versus the Giants on November 28, 2004, and his first 14 versus Green Bay on December 5, 2004, for a grand total of 24.)

Celebrate the Heroes of Pennsylvania Sports in These Other Releases from Sports Publishing!

Playing for JoePa: Inside Joe Paterno's Extended Football Family

Featuring interviews and profiles of 20 of the most famous families that have been part of Penn State football history in the last half-century, this book looks at everyone from the Suheys to the Bahrs, Sanduskys, and Paternos. 2007 release!

ISBN-13: 978-1-59670-176-2 • ISBN-10: 1-59670-176-5
$24.95 hardcover

Tales from Penn State Football

Readers are put on the 50-yard line with one of college football's most successful programs. From the first team in the 1880's to Joe Paterno's celebrated teams of the 20th century, Penn State's most entertaining and legendary football stories are chronicled. 2007 release! This is the first time this book has been available in softcover format.

ISBN-13: 978-1-59670-250-9 • ISBN-10: 1-59670-250-8
$15.95 softcover

Eagles: Where Have You Gone?

Fans get the inside story on what has happened to numerous Philly favorites of the past and where life took them after their playing days with the Eagles ended. The book includes looks at Pete Liske, Leroy Keyes, Super Bill Bradley, and many others.

ISBN: 1-58261-812-7
$24.95 hardcover

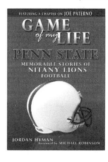

Game of My Life — Penn State: Memorable Stories of Nittany Lions Football

From Joe Paterno, talking about his first victory as Penn State's head coach in 1966, to Lenny Moore to Heisman Trophy-winner John Cappelletti, Game of My Life: Penn State: Memorable Stories of Nittany Lions Football is full of big names, big games, and 20 lifetimes full of memories.

ISBN: 1-59670-054-8
$24.95 hardcover

Tales from the Eagles Sidelines (updated softcover edition)

Gordon Forbes writes about the assorted cast of characters who have suited up for the Eagles, and who have thrilled fans with their talents and often-humorous exploits, providing new insights into the personalities of many favorite Eagles.

ISBN: 1-59670-153-6
$14.95 softcover

Pat Williams Tales from the Philadelphia 76ers

Former general manager Pat Williams writes about the 1982-83 NBA Champion Sixers and the transcendent talents (NBA MVP Moses Malone, superstar Julius "Dr. J." Erving, Maurice Cheeks, Bobby Jones, Andrew Toney) that made them special. 2007 release!

ISBN-13: 978-1-59670-117-5 ¥ ISBN-10: 1-59670-117-X
$19.95 hardcover

All books are available in bookstores everywhere!
Order 24-hours-a-day by calling toll-free **1-877-424-BOOK (2665)**.
Also order online at **www.SportsPublishingLLC.com**.